D1599476

Inquiry Dynamics

Science and Technology Studies
Mario Bunge, Series Editor

Philosophy of Science, Volume 1:
From Problem to Theory,
Mario Bunge

Philosophy of Science, Volume 2:
From Explanation to Justification,
Mario Bunge

The Sociology-Philosophy Connection,
Mario Bunge

Critical Approaches to Science and Philosophy,
edited by Mario Bunge

Philosophy of Science: The Historical Background,
edited by Joseph J. Kockelmans

Microfoundations, Method, and Causation:
On the Philosophy of the Social Sciences,
Daniel Little

Complexity: A Philosophical Overview,
Nicholas Rescher

Inquiry Dynamics
Nicholas Rescher

Inquiry Dynamics

Nicholas Rescher

Transaction Publishers
New Brunswick (U.S.A.) and London (U.K.)

Library of Congress Catalog Number: 00-020757
ISBN: 0-7658-0007-1
Printed in the United States of America

Library of Congress Cataloging-in-Publication Data

Rescher, Nicholas.
    Inquiry dynamics / Nicholas Rescher.
        p. cm.—(Science and technology studies)
    Includes bibliographical references.
    ISBN 0-7658-0007-1 (alk. paper)
    1. Question (Logic) 2. Inquiry (Theory of knowledge) 3. Science—Methodology.   I. Title. II. Series.

BC199.Q4 R47 2000
121' .6—dc21   00-020757

Contents

Preface

Over many years, my publications have explored various aspects of the methodology and conceptual technology of rational inquiry. The present book seeks to weave together some of these strands of thought regarding the processes and prospects of question resolution that are at our disposal.

A sensible treatment of limits and incapacities of knowledge-development must put the topic of questions in the foreground. For it is only when we consider knowledge in relation to the intractable questions that the strengths and limits of our cognitive resources can come to view. The issue of questions and problems will accordingly be highlighted here. Such a question-oriented treatment proceeds in the tradition of Immanuel Kant and stands in decided contrast to the knowledge-oriented approach that has been dominant in recent epistemology. For with René Descartes as their role model, twentieth-century analytic philosophers have been obsessed with the problem of skepticism and have therefore focused on the possibility of certain knowledge to the neglect of a concern for the issue of plausible question resolution which is, or ought to be, a critical component of the cognitive enterprise.

I am very grateful to Estelle Burris for her capable and conscientious work in putting this material into shape for the needs of the printer.

Nicholas Rescher
Pittsburgh PA
February 1999

1

Introduction

1. Preliminaries

It is misleading to call cognitive theory at large "epistemology" or "the theory of knowledge." For its range of concern includes not only knowledge proper but also rational belief, probability, plausibility, evidentiation and—additionally but not least—*erotetics*, the business of raising and resolving questions. It is this last area—the theory of rational inquiry with its local concern for questions and their management—that constitutes the focus of the present book. Its aim is to maintain and substantiate the utility of approaching epistemological issues from the angle of questions. As Aristotle already indicated, human inquiry is grounded in wonder. When matters are running along in their accustomed way, we generally do not puzzle about it and stop to ask questions. But when things are in any way out of the ordinary we puzzle over the reason why and to seek for a explanation. And gradually our horizons expand. With increasing sophistication, we learn to be surprised by virtually *all* of it. We increasingly want to know what makes things tick—the ordinary as well as the extraordinary, so that questions gain an increasing prominence within epistemology in general.

As long as we are concerned merely with what we know, the idea of limits of knowledge lies outside our ken. We cannot be specific about our ignorance in terms of knowledge: It makes no sense to say "p is a fact that I do not know" for if we know something in specific to be a fact we can, for that very reason, no longer be in ignorance about

1

it. However, "Q is a question that I cannot answer" poses no difficulty. It is thus only when we turn to questions—when we ask whether or not something is so in situations where we simply can't say—that we come up against the idea of limits to knowledge. Only as we come to realize that there are questions that we cannot answer does the reality of ignorance confront us. Accordingly, questions are epistemologically crucial because it is in their context that matters of unknowing—come to the fore. After all, we need information to remove ignorance and settle doubt, and "our knowledge" is constituted by the answers that we accept. What people know—or take themselves to know—is simply the sum-total of the answers they offer to the questions which they can resolve.

After the present chapter's preliminaries, the remainder of the book traverses the following ground. Chapter 2 explains the basic concepts involved in the abstract "logic" of questions and answers and sets out the generic fundamentals of this domain. Then chapters 3 and 4 expound the theoretical principles that characterize the field of question epistemology in general, clarifying the fundamental themes and theses of the subject. The ensuing chapters 5 and 6 explore the lay of the land of question epistemology within science, the most fully developed area of question-resolving inquiry at our disposal. The discussion here seeks to show that there are limits—restrictions of basic principle—to our ability to resolve scientific questions. And the next chapter, 8, argues that nevertheless, widely popular relativism notwithstanding, our questions about the world can be answered objectively and cogently. Throughout, it emerges that a question-oriented approach to the process of inquiry serves both to highlight the inherent limitations of the cognitive project and to substantiate its legitimacy.

2. Questions and Knowledge

Epistemologists are wont to see knowledge as basic. But this is problematic. They develop their theories via an elaboration of the relationship Kxp for "x knows that p." But they could just as well begin with the triadic question/answer relationship: "x appropriately accepts p as answer to Q"—symbolically $AxpQ$, seeing that a proposition is true if (and only if) there is a question that it answers correctly. Taking this perspective implements the critical idea that our answers to questions will, where correct, represent available items of knowledge. Any accepted item of knowledge p is, in the end, no more than an answer to the question, "Is it p or is it not-p that is the case?" Such an approach effectively coordinates the conception of knowledge with that of appropriate question resolution.

The aim of this observation is not to urge the employment of this somewhat cumbersome stratagem. It is, rather, to make the basic point that knowledge-acceptance and question-resolution are interrelated in a condition of conjoined significance. For questions and answers stand in reciprocal coordination: the statement with the inquiry that provokes it; the proposition with the interrogation. The epistemology of questions is every bit as significant as the epistemology of accepted answers.[1]

3. Questions and Answers

For present purposes it is thus a critical fact that there are not only epistemic principles about knowledge but also epistemic principles about questions. For example:

1. Which answer is appropriate will hinge upon just exactly what the question at issue is.
2. The viability (legitimacy, appropriateness) of a question depends on the availability of its presuppositions.
3. Not every (factual) question has an available answer.
4. No factual question can be resolved on the basis of logico-conceptual considerations alone.

The principal task of this book will be to consider some principles of this general sort and to examine their rationale and their implications. Its overall aim is to elucidate the epistemological dimension of the theory of questions and inquiry and thereby to illuminate the epistemological enterprise itself.

However, before turning to such epistemological matters it is useful to review some preliminary issues regarding the *logic and semantics* of questions.[2]

Questions are effectively requests for information. For all practical and most theoretical purposes one can equate the question "Is the cat on the mat?" with the request: "Pray tell me whether the cat is on the mat or not." And this means that answering a question is an act, namely, an act of meeting the request at issue.

Actions, of course, can be either appropriate or not. And specifically, a question can be raised meaningfully only where there are standards for assessing the truth—or at least the plausibility—of an answer. To raise a question to presuppose not only that it has an answer but that this answer is, in principle, determinable (identifiable). "What is an example of a statement that no human being will ever make?" is an absurd question. The demand it makes is one that cannot possibly be met.

A *rhetorical question*, by contrast, is one whose answer is a foregone conclusion. Such a question can be raised only at best and most for effect; its answer is so obvious under the prevailing conditions that there is no point in raising it. "Are there any questions?" "Can we ever answer any questions?" In the circumstances, such questions are trivial. Answering them involves zero cost and yields zero benefit.

Different questions can share the same answer. For example, "Hydrogen is the lightest element" would answer both "What's distinctive about hydrogen?" and "What element is the lightest?" An *explicit* (ostensible) answer to a question is one that once more echoes the substance of that question itself.[3] ("What's an example of an element?"—"Lead is an example of an element.") Such an answer mirrors the initial question. Not every (ostensible) answer to a question is an explicit one (the reply to the preceding question might simply have been "red"), but every question has such explicit answers. An explicit answer is always such that it can count as completely—but just completely—answering the question.

When actually different, albeit verbally similar, questions are at issue, their fully explicit answers will bring this fact to light. Thus "Why do owls hoot?" may mean "Why do owls hoot when they do, rather than keep quiet?" or "Why do *owls* hoot (whereas sparrows, for example, chirp)?" or again "Why do owls *hoot* (rather than, say, bark)?" In specifying the range of explicit answers, a questioner disambiguates the issue, and brings to light the exact question he has in view.

When an answer to a question is offered, the questioner need not, of course, be in a position to recognize whether or not this answer is *correct*. But the questioner should certainly be in a position to recognize that the proffered answer is a *possible* or admissible one that is apposite for the question at issue. One has not posed a well-defined question if one is not in a position to recognize the possible answers to it as such, that is, if one does not even know what is to count as an answer. A question is only appropriate when one is in a position to recognize its admissible answers—statements that afford feasible response, without necessarily being identifiable as *true or correct*. Such a range of possible alternative answers may be either finite ("Are elms deciduous—yes or no?") or infinite ("What is the melting point of lead?" or "What's an example of a calculus problem?"). Indeed, in principle this range can be all-inclusive and seemingly boundless ("What's Henry thinking about right now?").

It is important in this connection to note that statements of probability do not answer questions about matters of fact. "Why did the dinosaurs become extinct?" is *not* answered by responding "Probably because of a meteor impact" any more than it is answered by responding "A meteor impact possibly did it." For the question asks for what did it, not for what possibly or probably did it; those responses are answers to *different* questions. "Mt. Etna will erupt next year" is something quite different in cognitive import from "It is more likely than not Mt. Etna with erupt next year." The shift from statements of fact to statements of probability is a fallback position that we take when we cannot answer the question at hand and propose to substitute another that lies in its neighborhood. Accordingly, that probabilistic response is inappropriate in circumstances where definite answers are available and which rises to appropriateness only in circumstances where this is not the case. When we ask someone a question about probabilities we do so subject to the tacit presupposition that it is not feasible, in the prevailing circumstances, to determine the actual facts of the matter. To be sure, probability statements can certainly provide practical guidance. Will it rain or not? It may be that we just can't say. But if we know that rain is likely, that will be enough to induce us to take an umbrella. For the purpose of planning and action, probabilistic information is eminently useful, but the cognitive business of settling questions is something else again, since probabilities do not settle matters. So the long and short of it is that probabilistic considerations raise a set of issues that belong less to the epistemology of questions than to the theory of practical reasoning.

4. Issues of Taxonomy

There are two principal ways of classifying questions: by subject matter and by interrogative mode. The former is at issue when we distinguish mathematical questions from (say) geographical questions. With the latter mode there are (for example) such different question formulas as: why?, when?, how?, is it true that? what (would happen) if? what's an example of?, what is the best way to do? and the like. As regards other possibilities, it should be noted that—issues of formulation apart—there is not much point in trying to maintain a sharp distinctions between:

- *factual/informational questions.* (When was Julius Caesar born?)
- *practical/performatory questions.* (How does one skin a cat?)
- *evaluative/normative question.* (Is it better to learn dancing or drawing?)

Such a distinction is no better than superficial because these sorts of issues are so closely interconnected in their bearing and the issues concerned so intimately interwoven that drawing any hard-and-fast distinctions here is simply impracticable.

Questions also admit of evaluative appraisal in terms of different degrees of

- *difficulty* (effort-cost of providing an answer);
- *interest* (how it relates to the agenda that people have);
- *importance* (range of consequences and implications).

Difficulty is a matter of cost; interest and importance are matters of benefit (subjective and objective, respectively). The actual conduct of rational inquiry of course calls for balancing these off against each other as best one can, since answering trivial questions will make no real contribution to our knowledge. And it is clearly only when interest and importance are taken into account that answering questions will have any real bearing on the matter of cognitive progress. In the absence of such qualitative considerations the volumetrics of question resolution are pointless.

Notes

1. Philosophers of science, too, have traditionally emphasized issues of the confirmation and disconfirmation of theories into the neglect of the questions which those theories are designed to answer. An early and honorable exception is Mario Bunge, *Scientific Research*, 2 vols. (New York: Springer, 1967).

2. Regarding the former domain see Nuel D. Belnap, Jr. and Thomas B. Steel, Jr., *The Logic of Questions and Answers* (New Haven and London: Yale University Press, 1976). This book has a bibliography of the subject's older literature.
3. Belnap and Steel, following Harrah, call this a *direct* answer (ibid., p. 13). This terminology seems suboptimal, seeing that "direct" usually contrasts with "oblique" or "evasive" in this context.

2

Rudiments of Question Epistemology

1. Presuppositions

The dynamic dimension of question management deserves explicit emphasis. For knowledge in the wider sense is not something static—an unchanging set of known truths. It is the changeable product of an ongoing process. And inquiry is exactly that—a process that transforms one state of things into another.

Question-resolution is a matter of reduction by optimization—of singling out one best possibility from among a plurality of possible answers to a question. (*E pluribus unum* is our motto here as well.) And as answers come to light our questions themselves change—and the range of possibilities also changes. Inquiry, in sum, is a transformative process that changes one state of knowledge into another. And so, looking at the cognitive situation from the vantage point of question-answer dynamics is illuminating in itself and corrective in setting aside the misleading conception of a statically fixed "body of knowledge."

Questions always reflect the prevailing cognitive "state of the art" and arise in the setting of an existing body of putative knowledge. This contextualization means that it would be an illicit hypostatization to speak absolutistically of "*the* agenda of scientific inquiry" or "*the* body of scientific knowledge," without adding something like "of the late nineteenth century" or "of the present day." Such a caution is particularly germane when we realize that the "scientific thought" of *different* eras may well contain mutually incompatible contentions, so that their questions can actually conflict in having incompatible presuppositions.

A questionee always has three possible alternatives when responding to a question:

- to answer the question.
- to confess incapacity, admitting the appropriateness of the question but acknowledging an inability to answer it.
- to reject the question as inappropriate or meaningless, maintaining that the question is improper and has no answer (and here we have not ignorance but a rejection that must be based on knowledge).

But what is it that would justify making this third, rejectionist response?

A *presupposition* of a question is a claim (a thesis or contention) that is implicitly inherent in—and therefore entailed by—each and every one of its possible fully explicit answers. For example, "What is the melting point of lead?" has innumerably many fully explicit answers, all taking the general form "*m*°C is the melting point of lead." All of these agree in their common commitment to the claim that lead indeed has a (fixed and stable) melting point. This thesis accordingly emerges as a presupposition of the question. Again, the explanatory question "How does the moon cause an eclipse of the sun?" takes answers of the form "The moon causes an eclipses of the sun X-wise," and therefore presupposes that the moon does indeed on occasion operate so as to produce solar eclipses. Its presuppositions inhere in the very way in which a question is formulated: regardless of which answer we endorse, the presuppositions are something we will stand committed to in any case. Even hypothetical questions have presuppositions. Consider "How many angels can stand on the head of a pin?" To be sure, this does not presuppose the existence of angels; it merely asks how many angels could do so *if there were angels.* But it does presuppose that angels are the sorts of things that occupy space and time; physical beings can have a position of some sort.

The presuppositions of a question always engender yet further presuppositions lying "further down the implicational road" as it were. For whatever a presupposition of a question entails or requires is itself one of that question's presuppositions. Thus "Smith has a wife" entails

"Smith is a person," "Smith is of age," "Smith is male," etc. Seeing that (on the specified definition of the term) every logical consequence of a presupposition is itself a presupposition, it transpires that every question has infinitely many presuppositions, if only because p entails p-or-q. (It is not to be expected, of course, that a questioner would entertain all of them explicitly.)

The presuppositions of our questions reflect their *precommitments*: they constitute the formative background that we bring to the very posing of questions, rather than merely being something we take away as a result of asserting them. The propriety of a question is accordingly predicated on the availability of its presuppositions: a question whose presuppositions are not satisfied simply "does not arise." If Smith has no wife, questions about his ceasing to beat her are inappropriate. Similarly, if there were no such thing as a fixed velocity of light *in vacuo* (if this were something variable and circumstance-dependent), then it would make no sense to ask, "Can anything move faster than *the* velocity of light?" To pose or otherwise endorse a question is to undertake an at least tacit commitment to all of its presuppositions. Basing it on a false presupposition is just about the only way in which we can go wrong in asking a question.

It is a key fact that *all questions have presuppositions*.[1] For example, every question presupposes that it has some true answer or other. For *any* proposition p that answers a question Q will entail "There is some (true) proposition that is an answer to Q." To be sure, a question can be *virtually presupposition-free* in the sense of having only trivial presuppositions—those that are logico-conceptual truths. An example of such a question is: "Is it the case that p?" which has no presuppositions apart from those relating to its meaningfulness as a question. Again, "Are there any truths?" is another example, seeing that it presupposed nothing over and above "there can be truths—this is something possible."

Every question presupposes that it itself arises appropriately. For example, "Are there unicorns?" presupposes that it makes sense to look for unicorns, so that "There might be unicorns" is a presupposition of this question. If unicorns were not even a possibility, the question would not arise. Accordingly, various questions can have only minimal presuppositions. But by the time we remove *all* of its presuppositions, we have nothing left by way of a meaningful question.

A question can manage to be *trivial* in the sense that its very presuppositions afford an answer to it: "Are there meaningful questions?" for example, or "Does this question have an answer?" The answer to such a question is a foregone conclusion. There are also erotetic solecisms that involve a deficiency not in correctness but in awareness. This category includes any sort of self-answering questions, such as "Are there questions that take an affirmative answer?"

The status of a question is determined by the nature of its presuppositions. In particular, a *factual* question is one that has a contingent presupposition.[2] Since a presupposition to a question is implied by any possible answer for it, we thus have it that any possible answer to a factual question will be a contingent proposition. The legitimacy of our factual questions accordingly hinges on the background of available information. Where different presuppositions are available, different bodies of questions can be raised.

A "state of knowledge," or, for that matter, of *purported* knowledge—let it be $\mathcal{K}$—is always correlative with a body of questions $Q(\mathcal{K})$ that can be posed on its basis, that is, questions whose presuppositions it vouches for. Thus $Q(\mathcal{K})$ represents the question-agenda of $\mathcal{K}$. A question Q belongs to it if all of its presuppositions are forthcoming from $\mathcal{K}$, that is, if the question is appropriate relative to $\mathcal{K}$. The questions of $Q(\mathcal{K})$ are appropriately posable relative to $\mathcal{K}$-available concepts and K-available theses; each of these questions is such that its concepts are meaningful relative to $\mathcal{K}$ and all of its other presuppositions are $\mathcal{K}$-true.

As noted above, it is an illicit hypostatization to speak simply of the "body of scientific knowledge" without adding something like "of the late nineteenth century" of "of the present day." In the same way, it makes no sense to speak unqualifiedly of "the body of scientific questions"—no well-defined set of items is at issue here, in the absence of a particularizing delimitation. (Our symbol "Q" is not a variable with a particular range, but a notational device.) If one state-of-the-art stage in matters of knowledge, say $\mathcal{K}_1$, includes the proposition p among its commitments, while another, $\mathcal{K}_2$, fails to include p, then we can ask the rationale-demanding question, "Why is p the case?" with respect to $\mathcal{K}_1$ but not with respect to $\mathcal{K}_2$, where this presupposition fails?" When we change our mind about the correct answers to questions, we are also thereby at once involved in a change of mind as to the sorts of questions that can sensibly be asked. Discordant bodies of (putative) knowledge engender distinct bodies of questions because they provide

TABLE 2.1
Status Change of Propositions
(In the Transition from One State of Knowledge to Another)

	Before	*After*	*Description*
1.	+	?	fall into doubt
2.	+	–	change of mind
3.	?	+	discovery
4.	?	–	discovery
5.	–	+	change of mind
6.	–	?	ascent to possibility

Note: The three combination-possibilities ++, ??, and – are omitted here because no status-change is involved.

the material for distinct sets of background presuppositions. Accordingly, the state-of-the-art regarding questions is inseparably geared to the state-of-the-art regarding knowledge. When the membership of a body of accepted knowledge $\mathcal{K}$ changes, so of course does that of its question-agenda, $Q(\mathcal{K})$, the manifold of questions that can appropriately be asked on its basis. We want to know with respect to our knowledge both what questions it answers and what questions it poses. And this latter matter of what questions a body of knowledge opens up is one of the most pivotal issues of question epistemology.

One question may be said to *preempt* another when they have mutually incompatible presuppositions. Thus "When did Henry commit suicide?" and "Why did John murder Henry?" are at odds with one another in this manner. Conflicting bodies of assertions will always engender mutually preemptive questions—namely questions that respectively presuppose the contradictory propositions at issue.

In the change from one state of knowledge to another, a proposition can undergo six different possible modes of status-change, as set out in table 2.1, which signalizes the three conditions of affirmed, denied, and suspended (i.e., neither of the preceding) by +, –, and ? respectively. And, of course, as the state of knowledge changes, the status of the available question-presuppositions will change accordingly.

This fact that different bodies of knowledge provide for different questions in affording diverse bodies of available presuppositions of itself blocks what might be the accumulative view of scientific progress. Some theorists have maintained that science progresses cumulatively because its latter theories both (1) answer (and answer better) the questions answered by the earlier theories and (2) answer more questions besides. The progress of knowledge is simply a matter of fitting more pieces into the puzzle. While this view of progress can be criticized for failing to depict the way in which science has in fact progressed, the present line of thought also indicates that it has grave theoretical shortcomings. For it is clear that such accumulationism is undone by the simple fact that there are such things as changes of mind that involve not only additions to but also abandonments of the questions that we raise.

2. Formalism

A brief survey of the epistemological considerations regarding questions is in order. Some modest amount of formal machinery will aid in clarifying the ideas that are at issue here. Thus let $\mathcal{K}$, $\mathcal{K}_1$, $\mathcal{K}_2$,...continue to represent suitably characteristic bodies of knowledge and Q, Q', Q'' . . . to represent *questions*. And let the *answer set* of a question consist of the entire spectrum of its possible answers:

$\alpha(Q) =$ the set of all possible (feasible, ostensible, theoretically admissible) explicit answers to the question Q.

To say that a proposition p belongs to this set—symbolically $p \in \alpha(Q)$—is to assert that p provides sufficient information to answer Q. To understand a question is to be able to characterize its possible answers as such—and thus to coordinate Q and $\alpha(Q)$. For insofar as we cannot say of a statement that it does or does not count as a *possible* answer to a given question we do not adequately understand what that question itself is about. To be a meaningful question is to admit of a possible answer.

When true, the thesis $p \in \alpha(Q)$ states a logico-conceptually *necessary* fact so that we have $p \in \alpha(Q) \rightarrow N[p \in \alpha(Q)]$. Knowledge for present purposes is inferentially accessible knowledge, and we accordingly suppose that all knowers have access to logico-conceptual facts: $Np \rightarrow p \in \mathcal{K}$ for arbitrary $\mathcal{K}$. We thus have it that for all Q:

$p \in a(Q) \rightarrow (p \in \alpha(Q)) \in K$, for arbitrary K.

To indicate that the question Q has the presupposition p we shall write: $Q \ni p$. This can now be defined as follows:

$$Q \ni p \text{ iff } (\forall q)[q \in \alpha(Q) \rightarrow (q \rightarrow p)].$$

A presupposition is thus accordingly a thesis (proposition) that is implied by *all* of a question's admissible (explicit) answers, following from each and every one of them. The presuppositions of a question accordingly delimit the range of its admissible answers. Note that the mode of implication ($\rightarrow$) at issue in the final clause of this definition must be a strong one, lest things go awry. For example, if it were merely truth-functional or "material" implication ($\supset$), then the definition of $\ni$ would have it that every question would presuppose *every true proposition*.

Since presupposition is a purely logical relationship we also have: $Q \ni p \rightarrow N(Q \ni p)$. And, in view of the unrestricted cognitive availability of necessary truths, this again means that presuppositional facts are cognitively context-invariant: $[Q \ni p \rightarrow (Q \ni p) \in \mathcal{K}]$, for arbitrary $\mathcal{K}$.

A question that has a false presupposition has no true answers (and conversely). Such a question—one that rests on a false presupposition—may be characterized as *inappropriate*. (Addressed to a bachelor, "Have you stopped beating your wife?" would be an example.)

As observed above, every question presupposes that it has some correct answer or other. This can be seen from the fact that a truism results when the 'p' of the right-hand side of the preceding definition of ' is replaced by:

$$(\exists r)(r \,\&\, [r \in \alpha(Q)])$$

To be sure, it can turn out that this presupposition is false because the question admits of no true answer. It is then, of course, an inappropriate question.

We shall adopt the notation $p \,@\, Q$ for "p *(correctly) answers* q'' via the definition

$$p \,@\, Q \text{ iff } [p \,\&\, (p \in \alpha(Q))]$$

We now have it that for all questions Q:

$$Q \ni (\exists p)(p @ Q)$$

This definition of @, when conjoined with the preceding definition of $\ni$ means that a proposition is a presupposition of a question Q iff this proposition is a consequence of the mere fact that the question is answerable (i.e., has some correct answer or other). The preceding principle is instructively compared with the thesis that a proposition is true if and only if there is a question that it answers correctly:

$$p \text{ iff } (\exists Q)(p @ Q)$$

The question "Is p the case or not?" will always provide for what is required here.

We also now have the following theorem to the effect that an answer to a question entails all of its presuppositions:

$$p @ Q \rightarrow (\forall q)[Q \ni q \rightarrow (p \rightarrow q)]$$

The proof runs as follows:

(1) $p @ Q$ by supposition

(2) $Q \ni q$ by supposition

(3) $p \in \alpha(Q)$ from (1) by def @

(4) $p \rightarrow q$ from (2), (3), def $\ni$

(5) Our theorem follows from (1)-(4)

And this means that Q's having a correct answer—*any* true answer at all—entails that all of its presuppositions are true:

$$(\exists p)(p @ Q) \rightarrow (\forall q)[(Q \ni q) \rightarrow q]$$

For this follows at once from the preceding thesis and the fact that $p @ Q \rightarrow p$.

It is useful to draw some distinctions regarding people's ability to answer questions, specifically those between:

(1) x knows that Q is answerable—that it has an answer:
     $Kx(\exists p)(p @ Q)$

(2) x can answer Q, that is, he knows an answer to Q:
     $(\exists p)Kx(p @ Q)$

(3) x knows that p is an answer to Q: $Kx(p @ Q)$

Here (1) certainly does not imply either (2) or (3). But we have both
(2) → (1) and (3) → (2), so that (3) → (2) → (1). However (2) → (3)
need only obtain when Q is such as to have only one single unique
answer. Otherwise such a question as "Who is an example of a Presi-
dent who was assassinated?" provides a counterexample since here
one may know *an* answer without knowing *each and every* answer.

The salient lesson of these deliberations, however, is that questions
and answers stand coordinate with one another. A true statement must
be the correct answer to a meaningful question, and a meaningful
question is one that admits of a possible answer.

3. Issues Regarding the Legitimacy of Questions: Question Resolution

The Roman poet Pubilius Syrus long ago proffered the dictum that
"It is not every question that deserves an answer." Given any body of
knowledge $\mathcal{K}$ there will—as we have seen—emerge the set $Q(\mathcal{K})$ of $\mathcal{K}$-
legitimate questions, that is, of all those questions whose presupposi-
tions are assured by $\mathcal{K}$ (i.e., are all $\mathcal{K}$-members). Accordingly:

$Q \in Q(\mathcal{K})$ iff $("p)[(Q \ni p) \rightarrow (p \in \mathcal{K})]$.

When it belongs to Q(K) a question may be said to be *proper* or
appropriate with respect to K. Thus "Why is the moon made of green
cheese?" is an improper and illegitimate question (with respect to
what we ourselves know). So is a self-refuting question such as "Why
are there no questions that take an answer of the form: "Because..."?
This clearly rests on a false presupposition, one whose falsity is made
manifest by that very question itself. Unless the presuppositions of a
question are all satisfied, the question simply "does not arise"—*cadit
quaestio* as the Roman jurisconsults were wont to put it. On this basis

we have it that a body of knowledge will acknowledge as proper all questions for which it has an answer:

$$(\exists p)[p@Q \in \mathcal{K}] \rightarrow Q \in Q(\mathcal{K})$$

The converse, of course, does not follow: A question that is appropriate for a body of knowledge need not necessarily find an answer within it.

Questions with presuppositions whose truth-status is unknown or indeterminate—but none that are actually known to be false—might be characterized as *problematic*. To raise such a question in the prevailing epistemic circumstances is inappropriate because this would be *premature* since the whole question could well become undone by discovering the falsity of such a presupposition. For example, the question "Why is there anything at all?" if construed specifically as "What is *the* cause or reason for the existence of the world?" presupposes the viability of an answer of the form "*X* is the ground for the existence of the world." That is, it presupposes the existence of a single monolithic cause or reason for the existence of the (or a) world. But there is no assurance of this in the present state of our knowledge—seeing that existence could be the collaborative result of a potentially vast plurality of distinct and independent causes. Such problematic questions are, however, perfectly "proper" and meaningful.

However, questions that have *false* presuppositions cannot be asked correctly or properly: *every* one of their explicit ostensible answers is false, so that we encounter falsity whichever way we turn, with every possible explicit answer. An example of such an inappropriate questions would be: "Why did Henry eat the apple?" in circumstances where it was in fact Mary who did so. From the very start there is no hope of finding an acceptable answer to such a question. This is the case, in particular, with *indefinite* questions like "How long is a novel?" Any explicit answer—"A novel has length such-and-such" is going to be false. We can either respond to the question with another question "Which novel?" and, so remove the indefiniteness; or, alternatively, we can treat the question as ambiguous and reconstrue it—for example, as "What is the *range of lengths* of novels?" or "What is the *average length* of novels?"—so as to obtain a well-defined question.

The potential of question impropriety means that there are two ways of "resolving" a question: (1) by answering it, or (2) by dismissing it as inappropriate and based on an incorrect presupposition. Accordingly, a body of knowledge K resolves a question Q if it either answers this question or invalidates it.

To be sure, some questions—namely hypothetical ones—are based on false presuppositions that are (*pro tem*) *assumed to be true*. Such a suppositional procedure represents a perfectly meaningful process, but one that poses special problems that deserve explicit notice.

4. Hypothetical Questions

A hypothetical question (such as "Suppose Napoleon had won at Waterloo: Would he have invaded England?") is one that is based on an iffy proposition by way of presupposition. In the most radical case, such questions can actually be fact-contravening by making suppositions that we know to be false. Interesting though they sometimes are, such questions issue invitations to perplexity. Consider, for example, such questions as

- If the White House were in Paris, would it be visible from the Eiffel Tower?
- If Bizet and Verdi were compatriots, what nationality would Bizet be?

It is clear, to begin with, that these questions are, to all appearances, inappropriate on grounds of indeterminacy. For the range of what we actually know includes the following:

(1)   Bizet was French

(2)   Verdi was Italian

(3)   Compatriots are citizens to the same country.

These three propositions, taken together, entail

(4)   Bizet and Verdi were not compatriots

The hypothesis instructs us to accept not-(4). Since we have (1)-(3) actually entail (4) we must in the circumstances also abandon one of these premises. But that is *all* we know about the matter in the prevailing circumstances, apart from the consideration that (3) is hard to abandon since what is at issue is a matter of definition. However, the residual issue of whether it is (1) that is to be abandoned or (2) is circumstantially undecidable as a matter of principle. Since the question asks us to decide the contextually undecidable one way or the other, it is *ipso facto* problematic. The hypotheses at issue are just not informative enough to make a resolution possible. Thus compare:

- If Bizet were to have the same nationality that Verdi actually does have, what nationality would Bizet be?
- If the White House were located in Paris on the Île de la Cité, would it be visible from the Eiffel Tower?

Only with a good deal of supplemental information would such questions become tractable.

And the case of the second question is the same. For we actually know:

(1)   Washington is in the District of Columbia.

(2)   Paris is in France.

(3)   The District of Columbia is far distant from France.

and these entail:

(4)   The White House is not in Paris.

But the hypothesis instructs us to accept not-(4), while nevertheless giving us no clue as to whether it is (1) or (2) or (3) that is to be sacrificed: We do not know whether to relocate Washington on the Seine or Paris on the Potomac. The realm of fact is so coordinated and intertwined that fact-contravening hypotheses always engender perplexing unravelings.

In other cases, to be sure, the hypothetical antecedent requires no further elaboration because such elaboration could be irrelevant to the specific issue posed by the question. Thus compare:

- If Bizet and Verdi were compatriots, of what continent would they be denizens?

- If the White House were in Paris, would it be smaller than the Louvre?

Here the indetermination with which the stipulated suppositions confront us is irrelevant answering the questions that are posed since matters militate for the same resolution in any case.

The point nevertheless remains that certain hypothetical questions are flawed in that, as formulated, they admit of no definite answer. The hypothesis is simply insufficient to provide the definiteness required for a meaningful question.

The root of the difficulty with hypothetical questions is that fact-contravening hypotheses generally require more readjustments to reality than they themselves do—or even can—specify. "Assume the Eiffel Tower were in Washington D.C." But where? And how did it get there? And what are we to do with what it displaces? An unending cascade of questions ensues which cannot be answered from available information. The problems that arise here readily push matters into impropriety. Only by way of information-transcending postulations can one make sensible progress in this domain.[3]

5. The Knowledge-Relativity of Questions

As indicated above, a particular question Q belongs to $Q(\mathcal{K})$—the manifold of questions that can be posed on the basis of a body of knowledge $\mathcal{K}$—if all of Q's presuppositions are forthcoming from $\mathcal{K}$. The questions of $Q(\mathcal{K})$ are appropriately formulable relative to $\mathcal{K}$-available concepts and $\mathcal{K}$-available theses; each of these questions is such that all of its concepts are meaningful relative to $\mathcal{K}$ and all of its presuppositions are $\mathcal{K}$-true. The question-set $Q(\mathcal{K})$ thus represents the *erotetic agenda* of the body of knowledge $\mathcal{K}$—the entire manifold of questions that is authorized by it. Such an agenda suffices uniquely to determine the body of knowledge at issue and there is a direct correlation between bodies of knowledge and erotetic agendas. Specifically, all the following theses are readily established on the basis of these preceding definitions:

- If $\mathcal{K}_1 \subset \mathcal{K}_2$ then $Q(\mathcal{K}_1) \subset Q(\mathcal{K}_2)$
- $\mathcal{K}_1 = \mathcal{K}_2$ iff $Q(\mathcal{K}_1) = Q(\mathcal{K}_2)$

- If $\mathcal{K}_1$ and $\mathcal{K}_2$ are bodies of *putative* knowledge that are mutually incompatible, then there will be questions in $Q(\mathcal{K}_1)$ that $\mathcal{K}_2$ does not even allow to be posed.

Very straightforward arguments serve to establish each of these theses.

The correlation between erotetic agendas and bodies of knowledge is reflected in the fact that a body of knowledge $\mathcal{K}$ views a question Q as "answerable in principle" whenever it holds that an answer to this question indeed exists: $(\exists p)(p@Q) \in \mathcal{K}$. A relatively straightforward argument can be developed to show that such answerability stands coordinate with the knowledge-correlative posability of questions at issue in $Q \in Q(\mathcal{K})$. This result is the *Fundamental Theorem of Question Posability*:

$$Q \in Q(\mathcal{K}) \text{ iff } (\exists p)(p @ Q) \in \mathcal{K}$$

The proof runs as follows:

Stage 1

(1)   Suppose: $Q \in Q(\mathcal{K})$

(2) $(\forall p)[(Q \ni p) \rightarrow (p \in K)]$ from (1) by the def. of $Q(\mathcal{K})$

(3) $Q \ni (\exists p)(p @ Q)$ a general fact about presupposition.

(4) $(\exists p)(p @ Q) \in \mathcal{K}$ from (2), (3)

Stage 2

(1)   Suppose: $(\exists p)[(p @ Q) \in \mathcal{K}]$

(2)   Let the value of p at issue in (1) be p_1. Then by hypothesis: $p_1 @ Q \in \mathcal{K}$

(3) $p_1 \in \mathcal{K}$ from (2)

(4) $p_1 @ Q \rightarrow (\forall q)[(Q \ni q) \rightarrow (p_1 \rightarrow q)]$ as a general fact about answers. (See p. 6 above.)

(5) $(\forall q)[(Q \ni q) \rightarrow (q \in \mathcal{K})]$ from (3), (4)[4]

(6) $Q \in Q(\mathcal{K})$ from (4) by def $Q(\mathcal{K})$

Accordingly, a body of knowledge admits a question as legitimately posable iff it takes the stance that this question actually *has* an answer—though not necessarily one that it can itself provide.

A question is *open* relative to a body of knowledge $\mathcal{K}$ if this body sees the question as appropriate but is nevertheless unable to answer it. Accordingly:

$$\text{open}_{\mathcal{K}}(Q) \text{ iff } Q \in Q(\mathcal{K}) \;\&\; \sim(\exists p)(p \in \mathcal{K} \;\&\; p @ Q)$$

To see a question as answered is, of course, to see it as answerable. And it is, in fact, easily shown that $(\exists p)(p @ Q) \in \mathcal{K}$ follows from $(\exists p)(p @ Q \in \mathcal{K})$.[5] But, of course, the converse relationship does not hold. To pose a question is, in general, a far cry from being able to answer it. The thesis $(\exists p)(p @ Q) \in \mathcal{K}$ simply asserts that, according to $\mathcal{K}$, Q *has* an answer (is answerable in principle)—that Q is appropriately $\mathcal{K}$-posable, in that $\mathcal{K}$ sees all of its presuppositions as satisfied. But $(\exists p)(p @ Q \in \mathcal{K})$ has it that $\mathcal{K}$ actually offers an answer to Q—that there is some $\mathcal{K}$-relatively true proposition which (according to $\mathcal{K}$) correctly answers Q. One must beware of committing the quantifier-scope confusion that would be involved in conflating these two very different contentions.

6. Depths of Ignorance

Usually in epistemology we deal with knowledge. But its lack—namely *ignorance*—also constitutes a significant part of the subject. Now ignorance is simply an inability to deal with questions. Consider the following three possibilities:

(i)   We know the putative question Q that is at issue.
(ii) We know that Q is a meaningful question that actually has an answer. That is, we know $(\exists p)(p @ Q)$ and therefore know the range of possible answers to Q, namely $a(Q)$
(iii) We actually have an answer to Q; that is we know of some particular p that in fact $p @ Q$.

When we have (iii)—and thus (i)-(ii) also—then we are at the zero level of ignorance regarding Q. Over and above this, there are deeper levels of ignorance:

1st level: We have (i)-(ii) but not (iii); that is, we know of possible answers to our questions, but are ignorant at to the actual one.

2nd level: We have (i) but not (ii); that is, we know the question but do not know that it is an actually meaningful one, whose presuppositions are satisfied.

3rd level: We not even have (i); that is, we are ignorant about the whole issue. Here we know as much or little about the matter as Cicero knew of rocket science.

Where one reaches the third level of ignorance about an issue, things have come to be as bad as can be in cognitive matters.

Ignorance of the first level arises when we can grasp a question but, under the prevailing circumstances, are unable to answer it. (In Darwin's day of questions regarding the mechanism of heredity had this status.) Ignorance prevails at the deeper level of actual inaccessibility when we would not even pose the question—and indeed could not even *understand* an answer to it should one be vouchsafed us by a benevolent oracle—because presuppositions of undetermined truth-status are involved in such a way that the whole issue lies beyond the conceptual horizons of the day. It is not difficult to envisage present-day questions that exhibit the surface ignorance of level 1; any practicing scientist can readily give examples of this kind from the domain of his own research. However, the deeper ignorance of level 3 inaccessibility cannot be illustrated, except in historical retrospect. Nevertheless, the fact that *current* ideas went unrealized at *all earlier* historical stages is readily amplified to the speculative prospect that some intrinsically feasible ideas may go unrealized at *all* historical states whatsoever. For it is perfectly conceivable that some facts will never be recognized as such, and consequently that some questions—namely those which presuppose such factual claims—can *never* be appropriately posed. In human affairs the possibility of ignorance is pervasive, seeing that it can relate not only to facts but even to questions.

Notes

1. Compare the pioneering discussion of R. G. Collingwood, *An Essay on Metaphysics* (Oxford: Clarendon Press, 1949), chap. IV, "On Presupposing."

2. A proposition is *contingent*—in the presently relevant sense—if neither it nor its negation are logico-conceptually necessary. By contrast, it is cognitively contingent or (better) undecided when neither it nor its negation is known.

3. For further considerations of these issues see the author's *Hypothetical Reasoning* (Amsterdam: Reidel, 1964).

4. Taking the line that knowledge is *inferentially accessible* knowledge, we have it that $p \in \mathcal{K}$ and $p \to q$ entail $q \in \mathcal{K}$.

5. The argument for this contention runs as follows:

   (1) $(\exists p)(p @ Q \in \mathcal{K})$ by assumption

   (2) $p_1 @ Q \in \mathcal{K}$ for some suitable p_1 from (1)

   (3) $p_1 @ Q \to (\exists p)(p @ Q)$ by quantificational logic

   (4) $(\exists p)(p @ Q) \in \mathcal{K}$ from (2), (3)

3

Fallibilism and the Pursuit of Truth

1. Skepticism and Risk

Aristotle observed that "Man by nature desires to know." Our human situation in this world is such that we have questions and want—nay need—to have answers. Our commitment to the cognitive enterprise of inquiry is absolute and establishes an insatiable demand for extending and deepening the range of our information. In this cognitive sphere, reason cannot leave well enough alone, but insists upon a continual enhancement in the range and depth of our understanding of ourselves and of the world about us. But is this cognitive project realizable at all? We confront the skeptic's long-standing challenge that it is not. In their more radical moments, at any rate—skeptics insist that there is never a satisfactory justification for accepting any claims whatsoever. And the skeptical challenge to the project of empirical inquiry based on principles of cognitive rationality has a very plausible look about it. Our means for the acquisition of factual knowledge are unquestionably imperfect. Where, for example, are the "scientific truths" of yesteryear—those earth-shaking syntheses of Aristotle and Ptolemy, of Newton and Maxwell? Virtually no part of them has survived wholly unscathed. And given this past course of bitter experience, how can we possibly validate our *present* acceptance of factual contentions in a rationally convincing way?

The fact, however, is that the skeptic too readily loses sight of the very reason of being of our cognitive endeavors. The object of rational inquiry is not just to avoid error but to answer our questions, to secure *information* about the world. And here, as elsewhere, "Nothing ventured, nothing gained" is the operative principle. Granted, a systematic abstention from cognitive involvement is a sure-fire safeguard against one kind of error—those of commission. But, it affords this security at too steep a price. The shortcoming of that "no risk" option is that it guarantees failure from the very outset.

In any situation where risks are run and chances taken—inquiry included—two fundamentally different sorts of misfortunes are possible:

Misfortunes of the first kind: We reject something that, as it turns out, we should have accepted. We decline to "take the chance" and avoid running the risk at issue, but things turn out favorably after all, and we "lose out on the gamble."

Misfortunes of the second kind: We do "take the chance" and run the risk at issue, but things go wrong, and we "lose the gamble."

If we are risk seekers, we will incur few misfortunes of the first kind, but—things being what they are—relatively many of the second kind will befall us. Conversely, if we are risk avoiders, we shall suffer few misfortunes of the second kind, but shall inevitably incur relatively many of the first. Both approaches engender too many misfortunes for comfort. The sensible thing is clearly to adopt the "middle-of-the-road" policy of risk calculation, acting as best we can to balance the positive risks of outright loss against the negative ones of lost opportunity. The path of reason calls for sensible calculation and prudent management: it standardly enjoins upon us the Aristotelian "golden mean" between the extremes of risk avoidance and risk seeking. The course of reason is represented by a stance whose line is, "Neither avoid no court risks, but manage them prudently in the search for an overall minimization of misfortunes." Rationality insists on proceeding by way of carefully calculated risks.

Of course, no method of inquiry, no cognitive process or procedure that we can operate in this imperfect world of ours, can be altogether failure free and totally secure against error of every description. Any workable screening process will let some goats in among the sheep. And this general situation also obtains in the cognitive domain.

Now in matters of inquiry and question-resolution, the skeptic succeeds splendidly in averting misfortunes of the second kind. By accepting nothing, he accepts nothing false. But, of course, he loses out on the opportunity to answer his questions. The skeptic thus errs on the side of safety, even as the syncretist errs on that of gullibility. And the course of rationality clearly lies in a thoughtful endeavor to do the best one can, over all, within the constraints of one's situation.

The flaw of skepticism is that it treats the avoidance of mistakes as a paramount good, one worth purchasing even at the price of ignorance and lack of understanding. For the radical skeptic's seemingly high-minded insistence on definitive truth, in contradiction to merely having reasonable warrant for acceptance—duly followed by the mock-tragic recognition that this is of course unachievable—is totally counterproductive. It blocks from the very outset any prospect of staking reasonable claims to information about the ways of the world.

With our cognitive mechanisms, as with machines of any sort, perfection is unattainable; the prospect of malfunction can never be eliminated, and certainly not at any acceptable price. Of course, we could always add more elaborate safeguarding devices to the point of futility. (We could make automobiles so laden with safety devices that they would become as large, expensive, and cumbersome as busses.) But that defeats the balance of our purposes. A further series of checks and balances prolonging our inquiries by a week (or a decade) might avert certain mistakes. But for each mistake avoided, we would lose much information. Safety engineering in inquiry is like safety engineering in life: there must be proper balance between costs and benefits. If accident avoidance were all that mattered, we could take our mechanical technology back to the stone age, and our cognitive technology as well.

The skeptic's insistence on safety at any price is simply unrealistic, and it is so on the essentially economic basis of a sensible balance of costs and benefits. Risk of error is worth running because it is unavoidable in the context of the cognitive project of rational inquiry. Here as elsewhere, the situation is simply one of nothing ventured, nothing gained. Since Greek antiquity, various philosophers have answered our present question, Why accept anything at all? by taking the line that man is a rational animal. Qua animal, he must act, since his very survival depends upon action. But qua rational being, he cannot act availingly, save insofar as his actions are guided by his beliefs, by what he accepts. This argument has been revived in modern times by a succession of pragmatically minded thinkers, from David Hume to William James. Its threat is: If you want to act effectively, then you must accept something. However this is not the line that has been taken here. For the present position is rather: "If you want to enter into the cognitive enterprise, that is, if you wish to be in a position to secure information about the world and the achieve a cognitive orientation within it, then you must be prepared to accept something. Both approaches take a stance that is not categorical and unconditional, but rather hypothetical and conditions. But with the former the focus is upon the requisites for effective action, while our present cognitively oriented pragmatism focuses upon the requisites for rational inquiry. On the present perspective it is the negativism of automatically frustrating our basic cognitive aims (no matter how much the skeptic himself may be willing to turn his back upon them) that constitutes the salient theoretical impediment to skepticism.

Perhaps, no other objection to radical skepticism in the factual domain is as impressive as the fact that, for the all-out skeptic, any and all assertions about the world's objective facts must lie on the same cognitive plane. No contention—no matter how bizarre—is any better off than any other in point of its legitimate credentials. For the all-out skeptic there simply is no rationality-relevant difference between "More than three people are currently living in China" and "There are at present fewer than three automobiles in North America." As far as the cognitive venture goes, it stands committed to the view that there is "nothing to choose" in point of warrant between one factual claim and another. Radical skepticism is an H-bomb that levels everything in the cognitive domain.

In "playing the game" of making assertions and laying claims to credence, we may well lose: our contentions may well turn out to be mistaken. But, in a refusal to play this game at all we face not just the possibility but the certainty of losing the prize—we abandon any chance to realize our cognitive objectives. A skeptical policy of systematic avoidance of acceptance is fundamentally *irrational*, because it blocks from the very outset any prospect of realizing the inherent goals of the enterprise of factual inquiry. In cognition, as in other sectors of life, there are no guarantees, no ways of averting risk altogether, no option that is totally safe and secure. The best and most we can do is to make optimal use of the resources at our disposal to "manage" risks as best we can. To decline to do this by refusing to accept any sort of risk is to become immobilized. The skeptic thus pays a great price for the comfort of safety and security. If we want information—if we deem ignorance no less a negativity than error—then we must be prepared to "take the gamble" of answering our questions in ways that risk some possibility of error. A middle-of-the-road evidentialism of "doing the best we can" with our knowledge claims emerges as the most sensible approach.

As Charles Sanders Peirce never tired of maintaining, inquiry only has a point if we accept from the outset that there is some prospect that it may terminate in a satisfactory answer to our questions. He indicated the appropriate stance with trenchant cogency: "The first question, then, which I have to ask is: Supposing such a thing to be true, what is the kind of proof which I ought to demand to satisfy me of its truth?"[1] A general epistemic policy which would as a matter of principle make it impossible for us to discover *something which is* ex hypothesi *the case* is clearly irrational. And the skeptical proscription of all acceptance is obviously such a policy—one which abrogates the project of inquiry at the very outset, without according it the benefit of a fair trial. A presumption in favor of rationality—cognitive rationality included—is rationally inescapable. It could, to be sure, eventuate at the end of the day that satisfactory knowledge of physical reality is unachievable. But, until the proverbial end of the day arrives, we can and should proceed on the idea that this possibility is not in prospect. ("Never bar the path of inquiry," Peirce rightly insisted. The trouble with skepticism is that it aborts inquiry at the start.)

Such a "refutation" of skepticism does not proceed at the *item* level of showing that the skeptic's view of the matter is untenable in this or that particular case of purported knowledge. Rather, it proceeds at the *policy* level, showing the pragmatic superiority of adopting a systemic line of approach that is decidedly at variance with the skeptic's. Viewing the issue in this pragmatic light, we see that the skeptic's risk-avoidance policy is simply not one that is rational to adopt. It has to be recognized that any systematic cognitive policy that we could possibly implement in the real world is bound to allow some errors to arise. Given that errors can be of the two kinds we have been considering, there simply is no realistic way of averting errors altogether—all across the board. Now, the skeptic's problem is that his preferred stance ("Accept nothing!") represents a *particular* policy choice designed to avert errors of the first tried alone. Such an approach that is not only *not* mistake-proof, but rather a mistake-inviting, definite commitment of procedure—even though its only mistakes are those of the first kind. Viewed from the vantage point of representing a particular policy alternative, the skeptic's difficulty is that he avoids mistakes of only one kind only, without reckoning the overall price of maximizing those of the other.

To be sure, the argument against skepticism deployed here is thus at bottom also an essentially practical one. It does no establish the internal inconsistency or theoretical untenability of a skeptical position. Rather, it shows that the price we would pay in taking such a position is so high as to outweigh any real benefit that could possibly accrue from it. But this price is a price in the sphere of theory—in the area of understanding. That basic demand for information and understanding presses in upon us, and we must do—and are thus pragmatically justified in doing—whatever it takes to get it satisfied. Whatever the merits or demerits of skepticism as a logically tenable position, we are entitled on practical grounds to dismiss it unceremoniously.[2]

The only sort of critique of skepticism that makes sense to ask for is a *rational* critique. And, viewed from this standpoint, the decisive flaw of skepticism is that it makes rationality itself impossible.

2. Fallibilism and Its Implications

Still, the reality of fallibilism must be confronted on any such policy of rationally calculated risks. And in fact ample experience indicates that our efforts to secure knowledge all too often lead us into error. The fact is that in rejecting skepticism and running an evidentialist policy of accepting cognitive risks we must make corresponding adjustments in our conception of knowledge. If what we accept as knowledge is liable to error—if it is frequently or even occasionally in fact false—then we are constrained to operate a distinction between genuine and merely putative knowledge, the latter being that which we merely claim to be knowledge but which may actually turn out with the wisdom of hindsight to be no more than error. And so the stance that our own putative knowledge is genuine and that what we take ourselves to know is actually true has to be implemented with great caution. We are—of course—committed to seeing what we accept as knowledge to be true (we wouldn't be accepting it as knowledge were this not so. But we have to recognize that this is something about which we could be wrong, just as with so much else in this world. The price we must pay for avoiding skepticism is that of being "realistic" about the nature of our knowledge—of being prepared to see it in a fallibilistic perspective.

With any sort of estimate, there is always a characteristic trade-off relationship between the evidential *security* of the estimate on the one hand (as determinable on the basis of its probability or degree of acceptability), and its contentual *definiteness* (exactness, detail, precision, etc.) on the other. But technical science forswears the looseness of vague generality or analogy or approximation. It has no use for qualifiers such as "usually," "normally," or "typically"; universality and exactness are its touchstones—it declares not merely that roughly such-and-such generally occurs in certain sorts of circumstances but exactly what happens in exactly what circumstances. The law claims of science involve no hedging, no fuzziness, no incompleteness, and no exceptions; they are strict: precise, wholly explicit, exceptionless, and unshaded. In making the scientific assertion "The melting point of lead is 327.5° C," we mean to assert that *all* pieces of (pure) lead will unfailingly melt at *exactly* this temperature. We certainly do not mean to assert that *most* pieces of (pure) lead will probably melt at *somewhere around* this temperature. In science we always aim at the maximum of universality, precision, accuracy, and exactness. And this commitment to generality and detailed precision renders the claims of science highly vulnerable. We realize that none of the hard claims of present-day frontier natural science will move down the corridors of time untouched. Fragility is the price that we pay in science for the sake of generality and precision.

We learn by empirical inquiry about empirical inquiry, and one of the key things we learn is that at no actual stage does theoretical science yield a final and unchanging result. We have no responsible alternative to supposing the imperfection of what we take ourselves to know. (And there is no reason to see the posture of our successors as fundamentally different from our own in this respect.) We occupy the predicament of the "Preface Paradox" exemplified by the author who apologizes in his preface for those errors that have doubtless made their way into his work, and yet blithely remains committed to all those assertions he makes in the body of the work itself.[3] We know or must presume that (at the synoptic level) there are errors, though we certainly cannot say where and how they arise—else we would of course fix them.

The interesting fact emerges that fallibilism is a more plausible doctrine with respect to *scientific* knowledge than with respect to the less demanding "knowledge" of everyday life. Ordinary-life generalizations are such as to allow one who asserts (say) that peaches are delicious, to be asserting something like, "Most people will find the eating of suitably grown and duly matured peaches a rather pleasurable experience." Such a statement has all sorts of implied safeguards, such as "more or less," "in ordinary circumstance," "by and large," "normally," "if all things are equal," and so on. They are thus so well hedged that it is eminently implausible that contentions such as these should be overthrown.

In science, however, we willingly accept greater cognitive risks because we ask much more of the project. Here the objectives are primarily theoretical and governed by the aims of disinterested inquiry. Accordingly, the claims of informativeness—of generality, exactness, and precision—are paramount. We deliberately court risk by aiming at maximal definiteness and thus at maximal informativeness and testability. Aristotle's view that terrestrial science deals with what happens ordinarily and in the normal course of things has long ago been left by the wayside. The theories of modern natural science have little interest in what happens generally or by and large; they seek to transact their explanatory business in terms of strict universality—in terms of what happens always and everywhere and in all kinds of circumstances. We therefore have no choice but to acknowledge the vulnerability of our scientific statements, subject to the operation of the standard trade-off between the definitiveness of detail and its epistemic security. In inquiry as in life we have to be prepared to take chances.

3. The Pursuit of Truth

Given a fallibilistic insistence on the fragility and imperfection of human knowledge about the world's ways, one may well question the very idea of the "pursuit of truth." Considering that fallibilism has it that definitive answers to our questions about nature's modus operandi lie beyond our grasp, what actual work is the conception of *the truth* able to do for us?

The answer is: Quite a lot. To begin with, we indispensably require the notion of truth to operate the classical concept of correct assertion as "agreement with reality" (*adaequatio ad rem*). Once we abandon the concept of truth, then we would also have to abandon the idea that in accepting a factual claim we accept it as true, and thereby become committed to how matters actually stand ("how it really is"). The very semantics of our discourse constrains this coordination of truth and reality: we have no alternative but to regard as real those states of affairs claimed by the contentions we are prepared to accept as true. Once we put a contention forward by way of serious assertion, we must view its claim as representing, at the very least, our best *estimate of the truth*. We thus need the notion of truth to operate the conception of reality. By virtue of their nature as truths, true statements must state facts: they state what really is so, which is exactly what it is to characterize reality. The conceptions of *truth* and of *reality* come together in the notion of *adaequatio ad rem*—the venerable principle that to speak truly is to say how matters stand in reality, in that things actually are as we have said them to be. That is exactly how these concepts of truth and adequacy work, and they would not work out without that fundamental precommitment to the idea of truth. The very conception of inquiry as we conceive of it would have to be abandoned if the contrast conceptions of "actual reality" and "the real truth" were no longer available.

It thus follows that, in the second place, the nihilistic denial that there is such a thing as truth would destroy once and for all the crucial Parmenidean divide between appearance and reality. And this would exact a fearful price from us: we would be reduced to talking only of what we (I, you, many of us) *think* to be so. The crucial contrast notion of the *real* truth would no longer be available: we would be able to contrast only our *putative* truths with those of others but could no longer operate the classical distinction between the putative and the actual, between what people merely *think* to be so and what actually *is* so. We could not take the stance that, as the Aristotelian commentator Themistius put it, "that which exists does not conform to various opinions, but rather the correct opinions conform to that which exists."[4]

The third point is the issue of cognitive coordination. Communication and inquiry, as we actually carry them on, are predicated on the fundamental idea of a real world of objective things, existing and functioning "in themselves," without specific dependence on us and so equally accessible to others. Intersubjectively valid communication has to be based on the presupposition of a common attempt to get at the truth of things at least as much as the nature of our circumstances permits. All our ventures at communication and communal inquiry are predicated on the stance that we communally inhabit a shared world of things available for contemplation independently of any single person's ideas about them. Where we abandon the commitment to a commonly accessible truth in favor of our varying conceptualization—where we claim for ourselves the exclusive rights to conceptualization (where I conceive of my nightmare and you conceive of yours)—the question of reidentification (of whether your dream matter is the same one as mine) cannot arise, and so the prospect of a sharing of experience about them as such (i.e., as monsters rather than people's ideas about monsters) becomes impossible. It is, to be sure, perfectly possible for two people to communicate effectively about something that is wholly nonexistent and about which they have substantially discordant conceptions (for example, X's putative wife, where X is, in fact, unmarried, though one party is under the misimpression that X is married to A and the other that X is married to B). Given a shared commitment to an objective framework of things, such aberrations are possible. But this possibility itself attests to our standard commitment to a commonality of communicative focus as a basis on which alone the exchange of information (or misinformation) and the discovery of error becomes possible. The shared (conventionalized) intention to tell the impersonal truth about the same thing undergirds and sustains all our communicative ventures.

This points to a fourth important consideration. Only through reference to the real world as a *common object* and shared focus of our diverse and imperfect epistemic strivings for the truth are we able to effect communicative contact with one another. Our standard view of inquiry takes the line that the real nature of the world is, in the main, independent of the process of inquiry, one, however, that the real world canalizes or conditions. Dependency is a one-way street here: reality shapes or influences inquiry in its concern for truth, but not conversely. The truth is what we at least try to get at—however gravely our variable individual efforts may fall short. Our knowledge of the world must be presumed incomplete, incorrect, and imperfect, with the consequence that "our conception of the truth" must be considered to afford an inadequate characterization of "the actual truth itself." With respect to our cognitive endeavors, "man proposes and nature disposes," and it does so in both senses of the term: it disposes *over* our current view of reality, and it will doubtless eventually dispose *of* it as well. We must simply do what we can with the relatively feeble means at our disposal to estimate (as best we can) the actual truth of things. And we need the conception of "the real truth" to make sense of the inquiry-pervasive contrast between what we have and what we would ideally like to obtain.

The fifth consideration is that the very idea of inquiry as we standardly conceive it would have to be abandoned if the conceptions of "actual reality" and "the real truth" were no longer available to serve their crucial contrasting roles. We could no longer assert, "What we have there is good enough as far as it goes, but it is presumably not 'the whole real truth' of the matter." Without the conceptions of truth and reality we could not think of our knowledge in the fallibilistic mode we actually use—as having provisional tentative, improvable features that constitute a crucial part of the conceptual scheme within whose orbit we operate our concept of inquiry. For our commitment to the pursuit of "the actual truth" stands together with our acknowledgment that, in principle, any or all of our present scientific ideas as to how things work in the world, at *any* present, may well prove to be untenable. Our conviction in a reality that lies beyond our imperfect understanding of it (in all the various senses of "lying beyond") roots in our sense of the imperfections of our scientific world-picture—its tentativity and potential fallibility. In abandoning our commitment to an objective truth, we would lose the impetus of inquiry.

Inquiry, as we standardly conceive it, is predicated on a commitment to an inquirer-independent truth of things; it is a quest for information about "the real world" with respect to which our own conceptions of things are nowise definitive, and into which others can accordingly enter unproblematically. It is thus geared to the conception of an objective world: a communally shared realm of things that exist strictly "on their own," composing an enduring and impersonal realm within which—and, more important, with reference to which—inquiry proceeds. We could not operate the notion of inquiry as aimed at estimating the true character of the real if we were not prepared to presume or postulate a real truth for these estimates to be estimates of. It would clearly be pointless to project our estimates of the actual truth if we did not stand committed to the idea that there indeed is an actual truth to be estimated. The pivotal contrast in this regard is between "mere appearance" and "reality as such," between "our picture of reality" and "reality itself," between what actually is and what we merely think (believe, suppose, etc.) to be. And our allegiance to the conception of reality and to this contrast that pivots upon it root in the fallibilistic recognition that at the level of the detailed specifics of scientific theory, anything we presently hold to be the case may well turn out otherwise—indeed, certainly will do so if past experience gives any auguries for the future.

In summary, then, we need the postulate of an objective manifold of actual truth for at least six important reasons:

1. To preserve the distinction between true and false with respect to factual matters and to operate the idea of truth as agreement with reality.
2. To preserve the distinction between real and seeming truth, between appearance and reality, between our picture of reality and reality itself.
3. To provide a conceptual basis for intersubjective communication.
4. To furnish the basis for a shared project of cognitive collaboration.
5. To provide for the fallibilistic view of human knowledge.
6. To render possible our standard view of the process of inquiry.

As these considerations indicate, pragmatic considerations powerfully militate towards a commitment to the conception of truth and to its pursuit. For such a commitment will play a central and indispensable role in our thinking with respect to matters of language and cognition. In communication and inquiry alike we seek to offer answers to our questions about how matters actually stand. Our concern is with "the real world." It is seen as the epistemological *object* of veridical cognition, in the context of the contrast between "the real" and its "merely phenomenal" appearances. Again, it is seen as the target or telos of the truth-estimation process at issue in inquiry, providing for a common focus in communication and communal inquiry. (The real world thus constitutes the "object" of our cognitive endeavors in both senses of this term—the objective at which they are directed and the purpose for which they are exerted.) Truth and reality serve us as coordinated conceptions. And all these facets of the concept of truth are integrated and unified in the classical doctrine of truth as it corresponds to fact (*adaequatio ad rem*), a doctrine that makes sense only in the setting of a commitment to an inquirer independent reality and an actual truth about it. We stand committed to the idea that there *is* a truth of the matter even in circumstances where we do not *know* it. And indeed we could not acknowledge the insufficiencies of what we purport did we not have the idea of "the real truth" available as a contrast conception. In the end, a commitment to the pursuit of truth is rationally unavoidable in the context of our cognitive commerce with questions. The pragmatic utility of truth in the context of the teleology of inquiry is such that its abandonment is something that we just cannot afford to contemplate seriously.

Notes

1. C.S. Peirce, *Collected Papers*, ed. by C. Hartshorne and P. Weiss, Vol. II (Cambridge, MA.: Harvard University Press, 1931), sect. 2.112.
2. This discussion draws upon the author's *Scepticism* (Oxford: Basil Blackwell, 1980).
3. The Preface Paradox was initially formulated by D. C. Makinson, "The Paradox of the Preface," *Analysis*, vol. 25 (1964), pp. 205–7. For its analysis see the author's *The Coherence Theory of Truth* (Oxford: Clarendon Press, 1973), pp. 200–5.
4. Maimonides, *The Guide for the Perplexed*, bk., 1, chap. 71, sec. 96a.

4

Question Dynamics

1. Question Exfoliation

Human knowledge is not stable; it is a matter of phases and stages in an ever-changing state of the art, seeing that ongoing inquiry leads to new and often dissonant findings and discoveries. And the coordination between questions and bodies of knowledge means that in the course of cognitive progress the state of questioning changes no less drastically than does the state of knowledge. Alterations in the membership of our body of knowledge will afford new presuppositions for further questions that were not available before. Cognitive change inevitably carries erotetic change in its wake. The question solved in one era could well not even have been posed in another. As W. Stanley Jevons put it well over a century ago:

> Since the time of Newton and Leibniz realms of problems have been solved which before were hardly conceived as matters of inquiry...May we not repeat the words of Seneca...*Veniet tempus, quo posteri nostri tam aperta nos nescisse mirentur.* ["A time will come then our posterity will marvel that such obvious things were unknown to us."][1]

Questions cluster together in groupings that constitute a line of inquiry. They stand arranged in duly organized and sequential families; the answering of a given question yielding the presuppositions for yet further questions which would not have arisen had the former questions not been answered. R. G. Collingwood offered the following example:[2] To investigate profitably the question "Has Smith left off beating his wife yet?" we must disentangle it into subsidiary issues:

- Has Smith a wife?
- If so, was he ever given to beating her?
- If so, has he discontinued this practice?

These if-so sequences are such that, once started, each question presupposes an affirmative answer to its predecessor since otherwise these "later" question do not even arise. (It is possible to flog a dead horse, but not a nonexistent wife.)

There is accordingly a natural stratification in the development of questions. A question cannot arise before its time has come: certain questions cannot even be posed until others have already been resolved, because the resolution of these others is presupposed in their articulations. (Think here of the game of twenty questions—not until after we establish that a species of dog is at issue does it become appropriate to ask whether a large or small sort of dog is involved.) Inquiry is a dialectical process, a step-by-step exchange of query and response that produces sequences within which the answers to our questions ordinarily open up yet further questions. Such a process will issue in a regressive series illustrated by such exchanges as:

Question	*Response*
Is it the case that p?	yes-p
Why p?	p because q and r
Is it the case that q?	yes-q
Why q?	q because s and t

Although a register of this sort looks linear and sequential (as the temporal structure of human thought requires), the exfoliation of questions actually takes us into a treelike structure, with various components taking on a form akin to that presented in figure 4.1. The setting out of such a sequential "course of questioning or inquiry" always involves presenting a complex treelike or weblike structure of this sort. (Its transformation into a linear form in written or spoken exposition is a step which, however convenient, obscures the underlying complexities of the situation.) And as a well-designed line of inquiry unfolds it proceeds in such a way that the later questions are linked to the earlier ones in a means-ends relationship of subordination and follow-through in such a way that later questions pave the way for the ever more satisfactory resolution of their predecessors.

FIGURE 4.1
A Question Regress

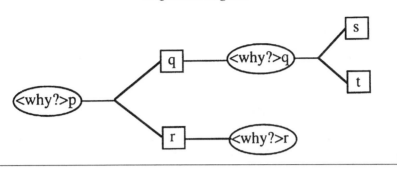

Structuring our information by seeing it in terms of responses to logically unfolding of questions is the most basic and doubtless the most important mode of cognitive system-building. To *systematize* knowledge is, in general, to set it out in a way that shows it to be the rational resolution of a rationally connected, sequentially exfoliated family of questions.[3]

Sometimes, to be sure, the direction of this means-ends sequencing, reasoning becomes reversed: To resolve Q_1 we must first answer Q_2 and to resolve this we need to answer Q_3, etc. In this way the operational tactics of inquiry frequently involve such "working backwards" from a given question to its erotetic prerequisites. But, of course, all of the questions in such a line of inquiry Q_1, Q_2, Q_3, etc. must belong to $Q(\mathcal{K}_i)$, when $\mathcal{K}_i$ is the then *currently existing* body of knowledge. In framing our questions (via their presuppositions) we cannot make use of information we do not yet have. In this regard, "working backwards" is a more restrictive process than the standard "working forwards," which generally carries us into new informative territory.

The unfolding of lines of inquiry defines the program of search—of research—that arises in question-answering inquiry, yielding a sequential process of question-and-answer where each A_i is an answer to Q_i. Once underway, we have in hand at each stage "a body of available knowledge" K_i to provide presuppositions for further question-posing, and it will always have to be the case that $Q_i \in Q(K_i)$. Accordingly, the circumstance that our answers to questions open the way to further question leads not only to regress but also to progress in the development of inquiry.

As experience shows, an answer to a question generally sets the stage for yet further questions by providing new materials for questioning. This leads to a cyclic process with the following structure:

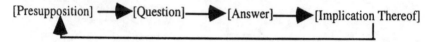

[Presupposition] ──▶[Question]──▶[Answer]──▶[Implication Thereof]

Such a cycle—an "erotetic cycle"—determines a *course of inquiry* which is set by an initial, controlling question together with the ancillary questions to which it gives rise and whose solutions are seen as facilitating its resolution. One question *emerges* from another in such a course of inquiry whenever it is only after we have answered the latter that the former becomes posable. The unfolding of such a series provides a direction of search—of research—in question-answering inquiry. It gives the business of knowledge a developmental cast, shifting matters from a static situation to a dynamical one.

It must be noted, however, that the dialectical exchanges of questions and answers can go awry through various technical defects such as circularity, vicious regressiveness, begging the question, or the like. Circularity, for example, is illustrated by the joke about the Eccentric Classicist: *Eccentric Classicist*: "*Why* should *anthropos* start with a *gamma*?" *Innocent Respondent*: But *anthropos* doesn't start with a *gamma*." EC: "Well then—why doesn't *anthropos* start with a *gamma*?" IR: "But why in Heaven's name should *anthropos* start with a *gamma*?" EC: "Ha—that's exactly what I wanted to know: Why should *anthropos* start with a *gamma*?" The formal structure of this exchange is clearly circular, and serves to illustrate that fact that a sensible line of questioning should always carry us into new ground.

The conception of a course of inquiry has important ramifications. For one thing, it helps us to see graphically how, as our cognitive efforts proceed, our questions often come to be seen as resting on an increasingly cumbersome basis, with the piling up of an increasingly detailed and content-laden family of available presuppositions. Moreover, it makes it clear how *a change of mind* regarding the appropriate answer to some earlier question can unravel the entire fabric of questions that was erected on this earlier answer. As further lines of questioning develop, our old answers can come to be seen as untenable and in need of correction or replacement. For if we change our mind regarding the correct answer to some particular question in the series, then the whole of the subsequent questioning process may collapse as its presuppositions become untenable. When people abandoned the luminiferous aether as a vehicle for electromagnetic radiation, they abandoned at one stroke the whole host of questions about its composition, structure, mode of operation, origin, etc. The course of erotetic change is no less dramatic than that of cognitive change regarding matters of accepted knowledge. Cognitive progress is commonly thought of in terms of the discovery of new facts—new information about things. But the situation is actually more complicated, because not only *knowledge* but also *questions* must come into consideration. Progress on the side of *questions* is also a mode of cognitive progress, correlative with—and every bit as important as—progress on the side of *information*. The questions opened up for our consideration are as much a characteristic of a "state of knowledge" as are the theses that it endorses.

2. Kant's Principle

New knowledge that emerges from the progress of science can bear very differently on the matter of questions. Specifically, we can discover:

1. New (that is, *different*) answers to old questions.
2. New questions.
3. The inappropriateness of illegitimacy of our old questions.

With (1) we learn that the wrong answer has been given to an old question: We uncover an error of commission in our previous question-answering endeavors. With (2) we discover that there are certain questions which have not heretofore been posed at all: We uncover an error of omission in our former question-asking endeavors. Finally, with (3) we find that one has asked the wrong question altogether: We uncover an error of commission in our former question-asking endeavors, which are now seen to rest on incorrect presuppositions (and are thus generally bound up with type (1) discoveries.) Three rather different sorts of cognitive progress are thus involved here—different from one another and from the traditional view of cognitive progress in terms of a straightforward "accretion of further knowledge."

The coming to be and passing away of questions is a phenomenon that can be mooted on this basis. A question *arises* at the time *t* if it then can meaningfully be posed because all its presuppositions are then taken to be true. And a question *dissolves* at *t* if one or another of its previously accepted presuppositions is no longer accepted. Any state of science will remove certain questions from the agenda and dismiss them as inappropriate. Newtonian dynamics dismissed the question "What cause is operative to keep a body in movement (with a uniform velocity in a straight line) once an impressed force has set it into motion?" Modern quantum theory does not allow us to ask "What caused this atom on californium to disintegrate after exactly 32.53 days, rather than, say, a day or two later?" Scientific questions should thus be regarded as arising in an *historical* setting. They arise at some juncture and not at others; they can be born and then die away.

A *change of mind* about the appropriate answer to some question will unravel the entire fabric of questions that presupposed this earlier answer. For if we change our mind regarding the correct answer to one member of a chain of questions, then the whole of a subsequent course of questioning may well collapse. If we abandon the luminiferous aether as a vehicle for electromagnetic radiation, then we lose at one stroke the whole host of questions about its composition, structure, mode of operation, origin, and so on. The course of erotetic change is no less dramatic than that of cognitive change.

Epistemic change over time thus relates not only to what is "*known*" but also to what can be *asked*. The accession of "new knowledge" opens up new questions. And when the epistemic status of a presupposition changes from acceptance to abandonment or rejection, we witness the disappearance of various old ones through dissolution. Questions regarding the *modus operandi* of phlogiston, the behavior of caloric fluid, the structure of the luminiferous aether, and the character of faster-than-light transmissions are all questions that have become lost to modern science because they involve presuppositions that have been abandoned.

And this brings us to the theme of fallibilism once more. A body of knowledge may well answer a question only provisionally, in a tone of voice so tentative or indecisive as to indicate that further information is actually needed to enable us settle the matter with confidence. But even if it does firmly and unqualifiedly support a certain resolution, this circumstance can never be viewed as absolutely final. What is seen as the correct answer to a question at one stage of the cognitive venture, may, of course, cease to be so regarded at another, later stage[4] Given the answer that a particular state of science S sees as appropriate to a question Q, we can never preclude the prospect that some superior successor to S will eventually come about and that is will then transpire that some different answer—one that is actually *inconsistent* with the earlier one.

The second of these modes of erotetic discovery is particularly significant. The phenomenon of the ever-continuing "birth" of new questions was first emphasized by Immanuel Kant, who saw the development of natural science in terms of a continually evolving cycle of questions and answers, where, *"every answer given on principles of experience begets a fresh question, which likewise requires its answer* and thereby clearly shows the insufficiency of all scientific modes of explanation to satisfy reason."[5] This claim suggests the following Principle of Question Propagation—Kant's Principle, as we shall call it: "The answering of our factual (scientific) questions always paves the way to further as yet unanswered questions."

Note, however, that Kant's Principle can be construed in two rather different ways:

1. A *universalized* mode: EACH specific (particular) question Q that can be raised on a basis of a state-of-knowledge $\mathcal{K}$ engenders a (Q-correlative) line of questioning that leads ultimately to a question Q' whose answer lies outside of $\mathcal{K}$—a question that forces an eventual shift from $\mathcal{K}$ to some suitably augmented or revised modification thereof.
2. A *particular* modes that arises when the capitalized EACH of the preceding formula is replaced by SOME.

On this second, more modest construction, Kant's principle can be formalized as follows:

$$(\forall t)(\exists Q)[Q \in \mathcal{K}_t \ \& \ (Q \text{ is new at } t) \ \& \ \sim\mathcal{K}_t@Q]$$

where we have: Q is new at t iff $Q \in \mathcal{K}_t \ \& \ \sim(\exists t' < t)Q \in \mathcal{K}_{t'}$.

On the first construction, science is an essentially divergent process, with questions leading to more questions in such a way that the erotetic agenda of successive stages of science is ever increasing in scope and size. This view was endorsed by W. Stanley Jevons, who

FIGURE 4.2
The Erotetic Dynamic of Inquiry

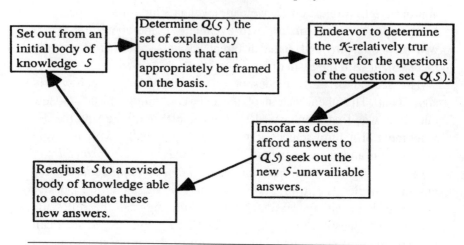

wrote: "As it appears to me, the supply of new and unexplained facts is divergent in extent, so that the more we have explained, the more there is to explain."[6] The second construction is, however, a far more modest proposition, which merely sees science as self-perpetuating with some new questions arising at every stage, thereby opening up a window of opportunity for the investigation of new issues. However, the question agenda of science is not necessarily a growing one, since questions may well die off by dissolution at a rate roughly equal to that of the birth of new questions.

Kant himself undoubtedly intended the principle in the first (universalized) sense. But it would actually seem more plausible and realistic to adopt it in the second, more modest (particularized) sense, which yields a thesis amply supported by historical experience: that every state-of-the-art condition of questioning ultimately yields, somewhere along the road, a line of questioning that engenders the transition. The states of science are unstable: the natural course of inquiry provides an impetus by which a given state is ultimately led to give way to its successor.

How can this principle possibly be established? What is at issue here is not, of course, simply the merely logico-conceptual point that whenever we introduce a new claim p into the family of what we accept, we can inquire into such matters as the reasons for p's being the case and the relationship of p to other facts that we accept. Rather, the issue pivots on the more interesting theoretical matter that new answers change the range of presuppositions available for new questions.

As we deepen our understanding of the world, new problem-areas and new issues are bound to come to the fore; as we have discovered, for example, that atoms are not really "atomic" but actually have an internal composition and complexity of structure, questions about this whole "subatomic" domain become available for investigation. At bottom, Kant's Principle rests on the insight that no matter what answers are in hand, we can proceed to dig deeper into the how and why of things by raising yet further questions about the matters involved in these answers themselves. Accordingly, whenever we obtain new and different answers, interest is at once deflected to the issues they pose. When physicists postulate a new phenomenon they naturally want to know its character and modus operandi. When chemists synthesize a new substance they naturally want to know how it interacts with the old ones.

Accordingly, the motive force of inquiry is the existence of questions that are posable relative to the "body of knowledge" of the day but not answerable within it. Inquiry sets afoot a sequential process, of a cyclic form depicted in figure 4.2. Here the body of "scientific knowledge" S and the correlative body of scientific questions $Q(S)$ undergo continual alteration. This process gives rise to successive "stages of knowledge" (with increasing t), together with their associated state-of-the-art stages with regard to questions, $Q(S_t)$. From a statically conceived "body of (scientific) knowledge," $\mathcal{K}$ or S, we are led to a temporalized K_t or S_t, indicative of the inherently dynamical nature of inquiry.

This Kantian principle of question-propagation in empirical inquiry indicates a fact of importance for the theory of scientific progress. One need not claim longevity—let alone immortality—for any of the current problems to assure that there will be no problems ten or one hundred generations hence. (As immortal individuals are not needed to assure the immortality of the race, so immortal problems are not needed to assure the immortality of the scientific frontier.)

3. Illegitimate Questions

It is convenient to adopt the convention that a body of knowledge S is said to *resolve* a question when S either *answers* or *disallows* this question. For any scientific framework for systematizing our factual knowledge is perfectly entitled to establish certain sorts of questions as improper—as "just not arising at all." Thus, when a certain form of motion (be it Aristotle's circles or Galileo's straight lines) is characterized as "natural" in a physical theory, then we are thereby precluded from asking why—in the absence of imposed forces—objects move in this particular manner. Or, again, considering that the half-life of a certain species of californium is 235 hours, we must not ask—given modern quantum theory—just why a certain particular atom of this substance decayed after only 100 hours. Such questions have presuppositions that are at odds with commitments of the body of knowledge at issue.

Membership in $Q(S_t)$ requires that the question at issue be a feasible one relative to S_t, but not necessarily that it be actually puzzled over and investigated by the concurrent practitioners of the discipline. Which questions are actually asked can be a contingent and often fortuitous reflection of the fashions of the day. Often, indeed, science assigns relatively little importance to a question until after it has been answered. Only after Rayleigh worked out his theory of atmospheric dispersion did the question of the blue color of the sky acquire much significance in optical theory. Only after Darwin's theory of sexual selection did the long-recognized vagueness of animal mating behavior acquire importance. In science as in life, there is much to be said for the wisdom of hindsight.

Its failing to fall within $Q(S)$ occurs when a question Q has a presupposition p that is unavailable for any one of the three reasons: (1) p is *false* relative to S (not-$p \in S$); (2) p is *undecidable* relative to S, as per claims about the mountains on the far side of the moon in the nineteenth century; or (3) p is *unavailable* in S because it is inexpressible within the conceptual resources of this body of knowledge, as happens with claims about the workings of the Galenic humors in modern biochemistry. We thus arrive at three corresponding modes of disallowing questions:

1. *Impropriety*, which arises when a question has an S-relatively

false presupposition. (In this case the body of knowledge at issue with *S* may be said to *block* the question at issue.)

2. *Problematicity*, which arises when a question is *indeterminate* relative to *S* and thus "presumes too much" involving an indeterminate presupposition—one that is simply not available on the basis of S-provided information.

3. *Ineffability*, which arises when a question has a presupposition that is conceptually unavailable in to *S*—one whose concepts *S* simply fails to envision.

A question that is disallowed by a body of scientific knowledge (in any one of these three ways) may be said to be *illegitimate* with respect to it.

Consider some examples. Present-day physics rules out as improper questions predicated on the realization of transluminar velocities or on the existence of a *perpetuum mobile*. Indeed, every purported law of nature rules out certain things as impossible; the acceptance of any generalization as a law of nature will block those questions based on conflicting presuppositions.

Problematicity is something else again. Given the present state of our knowledge, questions about the communication procedures of extraterrestrial inhabitants of our galaxy will be problematic: they are premature and "presume too far." Not just their answer but their very possibility is a moot issue. Yet they are certainly not improper—they are perfectly consonant with everything that we do know. But such questions can only be posed in the hypothetical and not in the categorical mode. ("If there are extraterrestrials, how might they communicate?")

Ineffable questions are not just *unanswerable* but actually *unaskable* because they cannot even be posed in the prevailing state of knowledge. We are not in a position even to formulate such a question—it lies wholly beyond the reach of the cognitive state of the art. Such questions can only be instanced through historical examples. Newton could not have wondered whether plutonium is radioactive. It is not just that he did not know what the correct answer to the question happened to be—the very question not only *did* not but actually *could* not have occurred to him, because the cognitive framework of the then-existing state of knowledge did not afford the conceptual instruments with which alone this question can be posed. Conceptual inno-

vation involves the formulation of issues that could not even be contemplated at an earlier juncture of the cognitive state of the art—and
may well abandon previously operative conceptions (for example, the
luminiferous aether.)

The history of science is replete with cases of this sort. In the main,
today's most pressing scientific problems could not even have been
contemplated a generation or two ago: their presuppositions were
cognitively unavailable. Every cognitive state of the art has its characteristic arsenal of conceptions which sets correlative limits that preclude certain matters from even arising and render alien issues simply
undiscussable. (Modern chemistry simply has no place of "affinity,"
nor modern physics for *vis viva*.)

We have already noted above (in chapter 2) that a state of science
can be identified via its question agenda

$$S = S' \text{ iff } Q(S) = Q(S')$$

It is easy to see that such identification obtains no less with respect to
answer manifolds than it does with respect to question agendas, so that
we also have:

$$S = S' \text{ iff } Q^*(S) = Q^*(S')$$

Here $Q^*(S_t)$ is the set of all those S_t-posable questions—members of
$Q(S_t)$—for which S_t also provides an answer, so that:

$$Q^*(\mathcal{K}) = \{Q: (\exists p)(p \in \mathcal{K} \& p @ Q\}$$

Where there are different answers there will, of course, be different
questions as well, since different presuppositions will then be available.

The fact that question agendas and answer manifolds each suffice to
identify an overall state of knowledge of course means that they should
coordinate with each other. It is to say that states of knowledge that
agree as to questions must also agree as to answers. Now, on first
thought this seems distinctly counter-intuitive. It might be said "Surely
the same body of questions can be answered differently, thus leading
to different bodies of knowledge. Surely questions underdetermine
answers." This seems plausible. But it only holds for *incomplete* bod-

ies of questions. A *comprehensive* question manifold will correspond to a similarly comprehensive body of knowledge. If K differs from K' even in the answer to a single question (say because K answers Q by p and K' answers it by p', then K admits the question "Why is p the answer to Q" whose presupposition is (by hypothesis) not available in K'. And so for the very reason that there is a question that they answer differently that two bodies of knowledge will differ in their declarative commitments as well.

Consider the following *Thesis of the Conservation of Questions*:

> Once posable, a question always remains to. A question that can be raised appropriately in our state-of-the-art in science will always continue to figure on the scientific agenda.[7]

This thesis to the effect that if $Q \in Q(S_t)$ then for any $t' > t$ we shall also have $Q \in Q(S_{t'})$ is something that is patently false. A presupposition of Q that is available at t relative to the state of science at that time, S_t, may fail to be available at t' relative to $S_{t'}$. Questions can be "lost" by being forgotten, but they can also be dissolved in the course of scientific evolution, when the scientific community comes to abandon their presuppositions.

Of course such a state of things does not means that there cannot be permanent scientific questions—questions which, once formulated, remain on the agenda of science for good:

$$\mathrm{perm}(Q) \text{ iff } (\exists t)(\forall t' > t)(Q \in Q(S_t))$$

First off, however, it must be said that that while scientific questions can be permanent they certainly are not necessarily so. All too often the presuppositions of one day are things that the science of a later day has changed its mind about. (The electromagnetic aether of Maxwell's day is no longer with us and the idea of a well-defined all-round "intelligence" measurable from a single-quality "intelligence quotient" seems to be loitering on its throne.) However, it can also be said that the more abstract and general a question is—the less it enters into matters of operational detail—the better its prospects of permanency are. "Why does water evaporate?" has been on the agenda of science since the days of Greek antiquity and can be counted on to continue. But "Why do all samples of (pure) water have the same specific gravity?" vanished from the scene with the discovery of heavy water.

The question-answering capacity of a body of knowledge should accordingly be assessed in terms not of *all imaginable* questions but on all the proper or legitimate questions, where the cognitive framework at issue is itself entitled to play a part in the determination of such legitimacy. When a cognitive corpus actually disallows certain questions, we cannot automatically regard its failure to provide answers for them as counting to its discredit. And in the light of such considerations, we cannot maintain that science can explain *everything*: the very most we can possibly claim is that "science can explain everything *explicable*; it can answer all *legitimate* explanatory questions"—where science is itself the controlling determiner of legitimacy.

The prospect of relative illegitimacy shows that the body of knowledge of the day not only delimits the assertions we can maintain, it also limits the range of questions we can appropriately raise. Immanuel Kant's *Critique of Pure Reason* was dedicated to the proposition that certain issues (that is to say, those of traditional metaphysics) cannot be legitimately posed at all because they are *absolutely* illegitimate since they overstep *the limits of POSSIBLE experience.*[8] The present deliberations pose the more mundane but nevertheless interesting prospect that certain questions are *circumstantially* illegitimate because they transcend *the limits of ACTUAL experience*, in that certain presuppositions of these question run afoul of the body of knowledge on hand.

To be sure, in scientific inquiry, as in all other human affairs, we have to proceed from where we are. Our confidence in the answers forthcoming relative to S_n—that is, S_t with $t = n$ for *now*, the state of the cognitive art that is currently at hand—should never be impaired by doubts that represent no more than a matter of "general principle."[9] The membership of S_n would not represent our best efforts at question-resolution if we did not see ourselves as committed to them: they would not represent *our* truth if we did not seriously regard them as representing our best efforts to arrive at *the* truth. And so, if S_n itself gives sufficiently powerful indications of p's behalf—so powerful as to indicate the ill-advisedness of expending further resources of time and energy in pursuing the issue—then we are quite entitled to let the matter rest there for the present moment. All the same, we must recognize that this is an essentially practical rather than theoretical position. The economic aspect comes to the fore here: Where the prospect of error is sufficiently remote, there presumably is no really *practical* point in expending resources in an endeavor to accommodate purely hypothetical worries.[10]

The fact that a day may come when we can do better should never stand in the way of our doing the best we can today. Rather, it should stimulate us to try to do better tomorrow. And so from dynamism we are led naturally to the theme of progress.

Notes

1. W. S Jevons, *The Principles of Science* 2nd ed., (London: Macmillan, 1877), p. 759.
2. See R. G. Collingwood, *An Essay on Metaphysics* (Oxford: Clarendon Press, 1962), pp. 38–40.
3. For fuller treatment of the relevant issues see the writer's *Cognitive Systematization* (Oxford: Basil Blackwell, 1979).
4. The progress of science offers innumerable illustrations of this phenomenon, as does the process of individual maturation: "After three or thereabouts, the child begins asking himself and those around him questions, of which the most frequently noticed are the "why" questions. By studying what the child asks "why" about one can begin to see what kind of answers or solutions the child expects to receive. . . . A first general observations is that the child's whys bear witness to an intermediate precausality between the efficient cause and the final cause. Specifically, these questions seek reasons for phenomena which we see as fortuitous but which in the child arouse a need for a finalist explanations. "Why are there two Mount Salèves, a big one and a little one?" asked a six year-old boy. To which many of his contemporaries, when asked the same question, replied, "One for big trips and another for small trips" (Jean Piaget and B. Inhelder, *The Psychology of the Child*, trans. by H. Weaver [New York: Basic Books, 1969], pp. 109–110).
5. Immanuel Kant, *Prolegomena to any Future Metaphysic* (1783), sect. 57; *Akad.*, p. 352.
6. W. S. Jevons, *Principles of Science* (op. cit.), p. 753.
7. Symbolically:

$$(\forall Q)(\forall t > t')[Q \in Q(S_t) \supset Q \in Q(S_{t'})]$$

8. Kant was perhaps the first philosopher to give serious attention to developing the theory of scientific questions and to exploit it as an instrument of epistemological method. See the author's paper on "Kant and the Epistemology of Question," in Jochim Kopper, et. al., eds. *200 Jahre Kritik der reinen Vernunft* (Mainz, 1981). However, Kant's initiative proved infertile, and the topic of questions long lay dormant until finally put on the agenda to twentieth-century philosophy by R. G. Collingwood. See his *Essay on Metaphysics* (Oxford: Clarendon Press, 1940).
9. Compare Chapters VI-VII of the author's *Scepticism* (Oxford: Basil Blackwell, 1980).
10. On this economic aspect of inquiry, see also the author's *Peirce's Philosophy of Science* (Notre Dame: University of Notre Dame Press, 1978), and in particular the last chapter "Pierce and the Economy of Research."

5

Questions and Scientific Progress

1. The Problem of Progress

How is one to conceive of cognitive progress? Is it simply a matter of more and more? Just exactly what is at issue here?

Progress in science is often characterized in terms of historical tendencies regarding question-and-answer relationships. Perhaps the most rudimentary theory of this sort is the traditional *cumulationist* view that later, more advanced stages of science are characterized as such by virtue of their *answering more questions*—questions over and above those answered at earlier stages of the game:

$$t_1 < t_2 \supset [Q^*(S_{t_1}) \subset Q^*(S_{t_2})]$$

This expansionist view of progress has it that later, superior science answers more questions, that is, answers all of the formerly answered questions (albeit perhaps differently), and furthermore answers some previously unanswered questions. Progress, according to this theory, is a matter of rolling-snowball analogous knowledge-accumulation: as science progresses, the set of answered questions is an ever-growing whole.

Along this line, Karl R. Popper has suggested[1] that if the "content" of a scientific theory T is construed as the set of all *questions* to which it can provide answers after current science has been readjusted through its inclusion to become $S + T$, then a scientific theory might be compared unfavorably with that of its superior successors—notwithstanding their substantive difference—because of proper inclusion with respect to this erotetic mode of "content." Popper asserted that, on this view, even though T_1 is assertorically incompatible with T_2, we can nevertheless be in a position to compare the question sets $Q^*(S + T_1)$ and $Q^*(S + T_2)$, and in particular, might have the inclusion relation $Q^*(S + T_1) \subset Q^*(S + T_2)$ that is to be indicative of progress. Progress, on this point of view, is a matter of enlarged question-resolution, of *answering additional questions*.

It is easy to see, however, that this will not do. For let p be a proposition that brings this assumed incompatibility to view, so that T_1 asserts p and T_2 asserts not-p. Then "Why is p the case?" is a question that the theory T_1 not only allows to arise but also presumably furnishes with an answer. So this question belongs to $Q^*(S + T_1)$. But it cannot belong to $Q^*(S + T_2)$, because T_2 (*ex hypothesi*) violates the question's evident presupposition that p is the case.[2]

Popper's approach accordingly founders on the fact that if one body of assertion includes the thesis p among its entailments, while another fails to include p, then we can always ask (as above) the rationale-demanding question "Why is it that p is the case?" with respect to the former, where the presupposition that p is the case is met, but now with respect to the latter, where this presupposition fails. Discordant bodies of (putative) knowledge engender distinct, mutually divergent bodies of questions because they provide the material for distinct background presuppositions. Modern medicine no longer asks about the operations of Galenic humors; present-day physics no longer asks about the structure of the luminiferous aether. Future physics may well no longer ask about the characteristics of quarks. When science abandons certain theoretical entities, it also foregoes (and *gladly* so) the opportunity of asking questions about them.

The reality of it is that in the actual course of scientific progress, we have not only *gains* in question-resolution but *losses* as well. Aristotle's theory of natural place provided and explanation for the "gravitational attraction" of the earth in a way that Newton's theory did not. Descartes' vortex theory could answer the question why all the planets revolve about the sun in the same direction, a question to which Newton's celestial mechanics had no answer. The earlier chemistry of affinities had an explanation for why certain chemical interactions take place and others not, a phenomenon for which Dalton's quantitative theory had no explanation. The cumulationist theory of progress through an ongoing enlargement in question resolution is patently untenable.

A second theory of progress takes the rather different approach of associating scientific progress with an expansion in our question horizon. It holds that later, superior science will always enable us to *pose additional question*:

$$t_1 < t_2 \supset [Q(S_{t_1}) \subset Q(S_{t_2})]$$

Scientific progress is now seen as a process of enlarging the question agenda by uncovering new questions. More questions rather than more answers are seen as the key: progress is a matter of question-cumulativity, with more advanced science making it possible to pose issues that could not be envisaged earlier on.

However, this second approach to progressiveness is also untenable. For just as progress sometimes involves abandoning old answers, it also often involves rejecting old questions. Paul Feyerabend has argued this point cogently.[3] New theories, he holds, generally do not subsume the issues of the old but move off in altogether different directions. At first, the old theory may even be more comprehensive—having had more time for its development. Only gradually does this alter. But by then "the slowly emerging conceptive apparatus of the [new] theory soon starts defining its own problems, and earlier problems, facts, and observations are either forgotten or pushed aside as irrelevant." This phenomena of problem loss invalidates the theory of scientific progress as question cumulation.

A third theory sees scientific progress in terms of an increase in the volume of resolved questions. Thus, Larry Laudan has argued against Popper that scientific progress is not to be understood as arising because the later, superior theories that replace our earlier ones answer all the questions answered by their rival (or earlier) counterparts, plus some additional questions, but rather simply because the replacing theories answer *more* questions (although not necessarily all of the same questions answered previously).[4] On such a doctrine, progress turns on *a numerical increase in the sheer quantity of answered questions*, that is, it is a matter of simply *answering more questions*:

$$t_1 < t_2 \supset [\#Q^*(S_{t_1}) < \#Q^*(S_{t_2})]$$

(Here the operation # applied to a set represents a measure of its membership.) But this position also encounters grave difficulties. For how are we going to do our bookkeeping here? How can we individuate questions for the counting process? Just how many questions does "What causes cancer?" amount to? And how can we avoid the ambiguity inherent in the fact that once an answer is given, we can always raise further questions about its inner details and its outer relationships?

Moreover, this position is unpromising as long as we leave the *adequacy* of the answers out of account. In its earliest, animistic stage, for example, science had answers for everything. Why does the wind blow? The spirit of the winds arranges it. Why do the tides ebb and flow? The spirit of the seas sees to it. and so on. Or again take astrology. Why did X win the lottery and Y get killed in an accident? The conjunction of the stars provides all the answers. Some of the biggest advances in science come about when we *reopen* questions—when our answers get unstuck *en masse* with the discovery that we have been on the wrong track, that we do not actually understand something we thought we understood perfectly well.

A fourth theory sees scientific progress in terms of *a decrease in the sheer number of unanswered questions*, that is, of *answering fewer questions*:

$$t_1 < t_2 \supset \{[\#Q(S_{t_1}) - \#Q^*(S_{t_1})] < [\#Q(S_{t_2}) - \#Q^*(S_{t_2})]\}$$

This approach sees progress as a matter of agenda-diminution. Progressiveness turns on a numerical decrease in the register of unanswered questions. But the same line of objection put forth against its predecessor will also tell against this present conception of progress. To be sure, the size of this gap between Q and Q^* is something significant—a measure of the *visible inadequacy* of a given state of the cognitive art. The striving to close this gap is a prime mover of scientific inquiry. But it is emphatically not an index of progress.

An increase in the volume of *unanswered* questions is compatible with a more than compensating increase in the volume of *answered* questions. A fifth cognate theory of scientific progress uses the *ratio* of answered to unanswered questions as touchstone and accordingly sees progressiveness in terms of a *decrease in the relative proportion of answered questions*:

$$t_1 < t_2 \supset \left[\frac{\# Q^*(\mathcal{S}_{t_1})}{\# Q(\mathcal{S}_{t_1})} < \frac{\# Q^*(\mathcal{S}_{t_2})}{\# Q(\mathcal{S}_{t_2})} \right]$$

But just why should one think this relationship to be essential to progress? It is perfectly possible, in theory, that scientific progress might be divergent, that particular increases in question-resolving capability might be more than offset by expanding problem-horizons. (Ten percent of 10^7 questions is still a substantially bigger than twenty percent of 10^6 questions.) In such circumstances, we could make striking "progress" by way of substantial increases in question-resolving capacity, while nevertheless having a smaller *proportion* of answered questions because of the larger volume of new questions. Then too, questions are not created equal. Clearly, one question can *include* another, as "What causes lightning?" includes "What causes ball lightning?" In the course of answering the one, we are called on to provide an answer for the other. Such relations of inclusion and dominance provide a basis for comparing the "scope" of questions (in one sense of this term) in certain cases—though certainly not in general. They do not enable us to compare the scope of "What causes lightning?" and "What causes tides?" (And even if we could, *per impossible* measure and compare the "size" of questions in this content-volume oriented sense, this would afford no secure guide to their relative importance.)

Some theoreticians have favored yet another, sixth theory—one that sees scientific progress as essentially *ignorance-enlarging*. That is, they regard scientific progress as a matter of *increasing the relative proportion of unanswered questions*. Thus, W. Stanley Jevons wrote:

> In whatever direction we extend our investigations and successfully harmonise a few facts, the result is only to raise up a host of other unexplained facts. Can any scientific man venture to state that there is less opening now for new discoveries than there was three centuries ago? Is it not rather true that we have but to open a scientific book and read a page or two, and we shall come to some recorded phenomenon of which no explanation can yet be given? In every such fact there is a possible opening for new discoveries.[5]

This theory sees scientific progress as a cognitively divergent process, subject to the condition that the more we know, the more we are brought to the realization of our relative ignorance. But this position also has a serious flaw. For it totally fails to do justice to those—by no means infrequent—stages of the history of science when progress does go along in the manner of the classical pattern of an increase in both the volume and the proportion of resolved questions.

Two further variant theories along analogous lines see progress as lying in increasing the proportion of answered questions or in decreasing the proportion of unanswered questions (i.e., ignorance reduction), respectively. For reasons closely akin to those already considered, these theories also have vitiating disabilities.

In sum, none of these approaches to progress through question-agenda comparisons offer much promise. Scientific progress will have to be characterized in different terms of reference. In relating the questions sets $Q(S_t)$ and/or $Q^*(S_t)$ at different times in the manner of the progress theories we have been considering one operates merely in the realm of appearances—how far the (putative) science of the day can go in resolving the visible problems of the day. And this whole approach is too fortuitous and situation specific to bear usefully on anything so fundamental as authentic progress. Apparent adequacy relative to the existing body of knowledge (which, after all, is the best we can do in this direction) is a very myopic guide.

The lesson of these historical considerations is simply that the perceived adequacy of science reflected in the relationship of question sets is a roller coaster that affords little useful insight into the fundamentals of scientific progress.

2. Quality Poses Problems

It is time to step back from the proliferation of doctrines relating progress to questions and view the matter in a wider perspective. The salient point is that even if the historical course of scientific inquiry had in fact conformed, overall, to one or another of the patterns of question-answer dialectic envisaged by these various theories, this circumstance would simply be fortuitous. It would not reflect any deep principle inherent in the very nature of the enterprise. For the common failing of *all* the approaches to progress that we have been considering is that they deal (in the first instance, at any rate) simply with questions as such, without worrying about their *significance*. To render such theories at all meaningful, this factor would have to be reckoned with. The theory would have to be construed as applying not to questions per se but to *important* questions—questions at or above some suitable level of significance.

Now, the "importance" of a factual question Q, where $Q \in Q(S)$, turns in the final analysis on how substantial a revision in our body of scientific beliefs S is wrought by our grappling with it, that is, the extent to which answering it causes geological tremors across the cognitive landscape. But two very different sorts of things can be at issue here: either a mere *expansion* of S by additions, or, more seriously, a *revision* of it that involves *replacing* some of its members and readjusting the remainder so as to restore overall consistency. This second sort of change in a body of knowledge, its *revision* rather than mere *augmentation*, is, in general, the more significant matter, and a question whose resolution forces revisions is likely to be of greater significance than one which merely fills in some part of the *terra incognita* of knowledge. However—and this is crucial—the fact of the matter is that the magnitude of the transformation from an earlier S_1 to a later successor S_2 can only be appraised retrospectively after we have actually arrived at S_2.

The crucial fact is that progressiveness, insignificance, importance, interest, and the like are all state-of-the-art relative conceptions. To apply these ideas, we must *already* have a particular scientific corpus in hand to serve as a vantage point for their assessment. No commitment-neutral basis is available for deciding whether S_1 is progressive vis-à-vis S_2 or the reverse. If the test of a theory is to be its problem-solving capacity—its capacity to provide viable answers to *interesting* and *important* questions[6]—then merely quantitative considerations that prescind from quality will not be up to doing the job.

This issue of quality is the sticking point. For the *importance* or *interest* of a question that arises in one state-of-the-art state is something that can only be discovered with hindsight from the vantage point of the new bodies of knowledge S to which the attempts to grapple with it had led us. In science, apparently insignificant problems (the blue color of the sky, or the anomalous excess of background radiation) can acquire great importance once we have a state-of-the-art that makes them instances of important new effects that instantiate or indicate major theoretical innovations. To reemphasize, the importance of questions is something that we can only assess with the wisdom of hindsight. Accordingly, to secure an adequate standard of progressiveness we had best look in an altogether different direction.

3. Applicative Efficacy as the Key to Progress

The most promising prospect here calls for approaching the issue of scientific progress in terms of *pragmatic* rather than strictly *cognitive* standards. As seen from the angle of such an approach, progressively superior science does not manifest itself as such, through the sophistication of its theories (for, after all, even absurd theories can be made very complex), but through the superiority of its applications as judged by the old Bacon-Hobbes standard of *scientia propter potentiam*—that is, through affording us increased power of prediction and control. This means that, in the end, *praxis* is the arbiter of theory. To understand scientific progress and its limits, we must look not towards the cognitive dialectic of questions and answers but towards the scope and limits of human power in our interactions with nature. For progress one must, in sum, look not so much to what we can *say* as to what we can *do*.

An instructive lesson emerges from these deliberations. On the one hand our capacity to answer questions is limited. But beyond this there is even a limited significance to the whole business of question-resolution. For even substantial success along these lines need not by itself betoken real progress in the project of advancing our understanding of how thins really work in the world. Instead, progress becomes manifest through greater power—in improved technology, if you will—so that its crux lies in enhancing the range of our practice. Successful application is the key: superior science is as superior science does when and as it establishes its superiority in point of its greater operational effectiveness. And it is thus in the field of action rather than in that of cognition, as such, that the power of improved science most strikingly manifests itself. The arbitrament of applicative praxis—not theoretical merit but practical capability—affords our best available standard for the assessment of scientific progress.[7]

Notes

1. Karl R. Popper, *Objective Knowledge* (Oxford: Clarendon Press, 1944), pp. 52-53.
2. Compare the discussion in Adolf Grünbaum, "Can a Theory Answer More Questions than One of Its Rivals?" *British Journal for the Philosophy of Science*, 27 (1976), pp. 1-22.
3. See Paul K. Feyerabend, *Against Method* (London: Humanities Press, 1975), p. 176.
4. Larry Laudan, "Two Dogmas of Methodology," *Philosophy of Science*, 43 (1976): 585-597. See also his *Progress and Its Problems* (Berkeley: University of California Press, 1978).
5. W. Stanley Jevons, *The Principles of Science*, (London: Macmillan, 1874), p. 754.
6. Compare Larry Laudan, *Progress and Its Problems*.
7. The author's books, *Methodological Pragmatism* (Oxford: Basil Blackwell 1977), *Scientific Progress* (Oxford: Basil Blackwell 1978), and *Empirical Inquiry* (Totowa, NJ: University Press of America, 1982), and *Limits of Science* (Berkeley: University of California Press, 1985), provide some discussions relevant to this chapter's deliberations.

6

On Learned Ignorance

1. Introduction

Authentic knowledge of the detailed truth of things is by nature something of an idealization: it is what emerges from appropriate inquiry appropriately carried through. As such, there is nothing relative about it: the truth is the same for one as for another. But this world of ours is such that we unfortunately do not operate in ideal circumstances. After all, our circumstances differ in point of experience and evidence. And so what we do get—and all that we in fact can get—are *our best estimates* of the truth. And here as in other contexts estimation can be off the mark. So how can we escape from the relativism of a conflicting mass of individual opinions? Must we not abandon "the pursuit of truth" as no more than a quest for the unattainable?

The answer here lies in going back to basics. Rationality requires of us that in pursuing our goals we do the best that we can with the resources at our disposal. And this is the case in inquiry even as elsewhere. In the pursuit of truth we must do the best we can. Rationality insists that we do no less. But it also acknowledges that we can do no more.

To be sure, the question lurks: Is the best we can do actually good enough? Does doing our best guarantee reaching the goal in matters of question resolution? The answer here is: clearly not. In inquiry, as elsewhere, we often fall short. There are no guarantees in the pursuit of truth. Seldom does the science of the day endorse fully and unqualifiedly the science of an earlier generation. This is a fact of life that we have to take in stride. And it affords no reason whatever for abstaining from doing the best that we can. By hypothesis no more advantageous prospect lies before us.

But if we acknowledge our cognitive fallibilism, then what entitles us to stake those cognitive claims that we make—to accept all those contentions that we actually endorse? To see what is at issue here, we do best by noting that those truth-claims of ours are just exactly that: *our best estimates of the truth.* And it lies in the very nature of rational estimates as such that we are entitled to cast them in the role of the items that they are estimates of. They would not *be* our best estimates if we were not entitled to view them as appropriate operational surrogates for the estimation-targets at issue. There is nothing specifically relative about "my truth"—it would not be what it is if I did not take it to be *the* truth.

Of course we can go wrong in matters of truth estimation. Here, as elsewhere in this imperfect world, there are no categorical guarantees. But while guarantees are missing, there are two powerfully assuring considerations. The first is that if any extensive success in goal attainment in cognitive contexts is realizable at all, then this is the way to achieve it. The second is that in so proceeding we manage—as best we can tell—to proceed successfully in matters of goal attainment: that this is the best prospect that we have. And so the crucial point is that in doing the best one can one proceeds appropriately through doing the most that anyone—ourselves included—can reasonably ask of us. (*Ultra posse nemo obligatur,* as the Roman jurisconsults had it.)

The fact that we can never resolve all of our questions means that we must come to terms with the unavoidability of ignorance. Just how serious a liability does this constitute?

Although ignorance lies at the core of the present discussion, it is not an exercise in radical skepticism. It will not take the pessimistic line of a cognitive negativism to the effect that knowledge about the world—and indeed every rational well-founded beliefs about it—is unachievable. On the contrary, the present approach is one of cautious optimism, arguing that while reliable information is often not as easy to achieve as people incline to think, the cognitive enterprise can successfully come to terms with this fact. Evolutionary considerations afford us good reason to think that we live in a "user-friendly" world where we do not need to be right about things for our opinion-guided action to be successful. And indeed even in cognitive matters we can—strange to say—manage to extract truth from error. Let us see how this comes to be.

2. The Vagaries of Vagueness

One fundamental feature of inquiry is represented by the following observation:

THESIS 1: *Insofar as our thinking is vague, truth is accessible even in the face of error.*

Consider the situation where you correctly accept *P*-or-*Q*. But—so let it be supposed—the truth of this disjunction roots entirely in that of *P* while *Q* is quite false. However, you accept *P*-or-*Q* only because you are convinced of the truth of *Q*; it so happens that *P* is something you actually disbelieve. Yet despite your error, your belief is entirely true.[1] Consider a concrete instance. You believe that Mr. Kim Ho is Korean because you believe him to be a North Korean. However he is, in fact a South Korean, something you would flatly reject. Nevertheless your belief that he is Korean is unquestionably correct. The error in which you are involved, although real, is not so grave as to destabilize the truth of your belief.

This example illustrates a more far-reaching point.

THESIS 2: *There is, in general, an inverse relationship between the precision or definiteness of a judgment and its security: detail and probability stand in a competing relationship.*

Increased confidence in the correctness of our estimates can always be purchased at the price of decreased accuracy. We estimate the height of the tree at *around* 25 feet. We are *quite sure* that the tree is 25±5 feet high. We are *virtually certain* that its height is 25±10 feet. But we can be *completely and absolutely sure* that its height is between 1 inch and 100 yards. Of this we can be "completely sure" in the sense that we are "absolutely certain," "certain beyond the shadow of a doubt," "as certain as we can be of anything in the world," "so sure that we would be willing to stake your life on it," and the like. For any sort of estimate whatsoever there is always a characteristic

FIGURE 6.1
The Trade-Off Between Security and Definiteness in Estimation

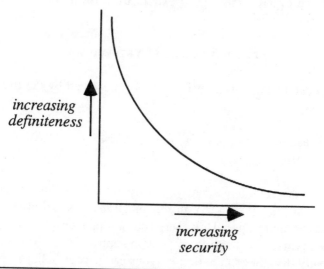

Note: Given suitable ways of measuring security (*s* and definitiveness (*d*), the curve at issue can be supposed to be the equilateral hyperbola: $s \times d = $ constant.

trade-off relationship between the evidential *security* of the estimate, on the one hand (as determinable on the basis of its probability or degree of acceptability), and on the other hand its contentual *definitiveness* (exactness, detail, precision, etc.). A situation of the sort depicted by the curve of figure 6.1 obtains with the result that a *complementarity* relationship of sorts obtains here as between definiteness and security.[2]

And this state of affairs has far-reaching consequences. It means, in particular, that no secure statement about reality can say exactly how matters stand universally always and everywhere. To capture the truth of things by means of language we must proceed by way of "warranted approximation." In general we can be sure of how things "usually" are and how they "roughly" are, but not how they always and exactly are.

The moral of this story is that, insofar as our ignorance of relevant matters leads us to be vague in our judgments, we may well manage to enhance the likelihood of being right. The fact of the matter is that we have:

THESIS 3: *By constraining us to make vaguer judgments, ignorance enhances our access to correct information (albeit at the cost of less detail and precision).*

Thus if I have forgotten that Seattle is in Washington State, then if "forced to guess" I might well erroneously locate it in Oregon. Nevertheless, my vague judgment that "Seattle is located in the Northwestern U.S." is quite correct. This state of affairs means that when the truth of our claims is critical we generally "play it safe" and make our commitments less definite and detailed.

Consider, for example, so simple and colloquial a statement as "The servant declared that he could no longer do his master's bidding." This statement is pervaded by a magisterial vagueness. It conveys very little about what went on in the exchange between servant and master. We are told virtually nothing about what either of them actually said. What the object of their discussion was, what form of words they used, the manner of their discourse (did the master order or request, was the servant speaking from rueful incapacity or from belligerent defiance) all these are questions we cannot begin to answer. Even the relationship at issue, whether owner/slave or employer/employee is left in total obscurity. In sum, there is a vast range of indeterminacy here—a great multitude of very different scenarios would fit perfectly well to the description of events which that individual statement puts before us. And this vagueness clearly provides a protective shell to guard that statement against a charge of falsity. Irrespective of how matters might actually stand within a vast range of alternatives, the statement remains secure, its truth unaffected by which possibility is realized.

And in practical matters such rough guidance is often altogether enough. We need not know just how much rain there will be to make it sensible for us to take an umbrella.

3. Cognitive Risk

In view of the preceding consideration we also have:

THESIS 4: *In practice our beliefs are generally overdetermined by the evidence. In order "to be sure," we generally "overdesign" our beliefs in matters that are important to us by keeping them comparatively indefinite.*

Engineers standardly overdesign their productions. They build the bridge to bear more weight than will conceivably ever be placed upon it; they build the dam to withstand far more pressure than the reservoir is expected to exert. Analogously, our beliefs—especially in matters of importance—are generally such that the relevant evidence at our disposal would in fact support something far stronger. Where error avoidance is an issue our beliefs are usually so "overdesigned" that the evidence actually at our disposal would, in fact, support weightier and more content-laden claims.

All the same, it is clear that risk avoidance in matters of belief stands coordinate with skepticism. The skeptic's line is: Run no risk of error; take no chances; accept nothing that does not come with totally ironclad guarantees. And the proviso here is largely academic, seeing that little if anything in this world comes with ironclad guarantees—certainly nothing by way of interesting knowledge.

It must, however, be recognized that in general two fundamentally different kinds of misfortunes are possible in cognitive situations where risks are run and chances taken:

1. *Omission errors*: We reject something that, as it turns out, we should have accepted. We decline to take the chance, we avoid running the risk at issue, but things turn out favorably after all, so that we lose out on the gamble.
2. *Commission errors:* We accept something that, as it turns out, we should have rejected. We do take the chance and run the risk at issue, but things go wrong, so that we lose the gamble.

If we are risk seekers, we will incur few misfortunes of the first kind, but, things being what they are, many of the second kind well befall us. On the other hand, if we are risk avoiders, we shall suffer few misfortunes of the second kind, but shall inevitably incur many of the first. The overall situation has the general structure depicted in figure 6.2.

Clearly, the reasonable thing to do is to adopt a policy that minimizes misfortunes overall. And this means that a rigid policy of avoiding all errors of a given type (be it omission or commission) will, in general, fail to be rationally optimal. Both approaches engender too many misfortunes for comfort. The sensible and prudent thing is to adopt the middle-of-the-road policy of risk calculation, striving as best

FIGURE 6.2
The Cost of Risk Managfement Approaches

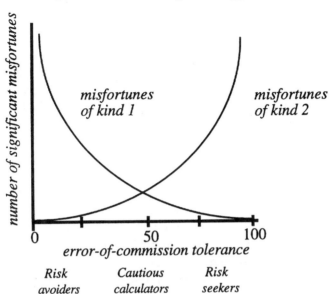

we can to balance the positive risks of outright loss against the negative ones of lost opportunity. The rule of reason calls for sensible management and a prudent calculation of risks; it standardly enjoins upon us the Aristotelian golden mean between the extreme of risk avoidance and risk seeking.

Turning now to the specifically cognitive case, it may be observed that the skeptic succeeds splendidly in averting misfortunes of the second kind. He makes no errors of commission; by accepting nothing, he accepts nothing false. But, of course, he loses out on the opportunity to obtain any sort of information. The skeptic thus errs on the side of safety, even as the syncretist errs on that of gullibility. The sensible course is clearly that of a prudent calculation of risks. As William James stressed, the only sensible attitude is that of the stance: "Certainly the cognitive enterprise has its risks, but we must be prepared to run them."

Ultimately, we face a question of tradeoffs. Are we prepared to run a greater risk of mistakes to secure the potential benefit of an enlarged understanding? In the end, the matter is one of priorities—of safety as against information and of an epistemological risk aversion as against the impetus to understanding. The ultimate issue is one of values and priorities, weighing the negativity of ignorance and incomprehension against the risk of mistakes and misinformation. But for each mistake avoided, we would lose much information. Safety engineering in inquiry is like safety engineering in life. There must be proper balance between costs and benefits.

All the same there is only so much that we can do by way of controlling cognitive vistas. We live in a world without easy options—and without guarantees.

4. Fuller Information does not Assure Safety

Herbert Spencer is said to have quipped that Thomas Buckle's idea of a tragedy was an elegant theory killed off by a recalcitrant fact. And it is clear that any belief, no matter how amply confirmed, can be destroyed by an unexpected encounter with an inconveniently nonconforming fact. A single black swan refutes the thesis that "All swans are white."

Nevertheless, one of the deepest ironies of the epistemic realm is represented by:

THESIS 5: *It would be an error to think that a conclusion based on fuller information is necessarily an improvement, presenting us with a result that cannot be false if its "inferior" predecessor was already true.*

If the belief at issue were true, then as more information is added, an outcome's probability would increasingly move in the same direction, and could not oscillate between increases and decreases. But this is clearly not so. Consider the following example, based on the question:

What will John do to occupy himself on the trip?

Suppose we require an answer to this question. But suppose further that the following data becomes successively available:

(1)   He loves doing crosswords;
(2)   He loves reading mysteries even more;
(3)   He didn't take any books along.

It is clear that we are led to and fro. Initially (at stage (1) of information access) we incline to the answer that he will be working crosswords. At the next stage, when item (2) arrives we change our mind and incline to the answer that he will be reading. At stage (3) we abandon this situation and go back to our initial view. And of course a subsequent stage, say one where we have

(4)   One of this fellow passengers lends him a book.

can reverse the situation and return matters to step (2). And who know what step (5) will bring? The crucial point is that additional information need not necessarily serve to settle matters by bringing us closer to the truth.

Consider a somewhat more general example. Suppose a sequence of concentric circles each of which has half the radius of its predecessor. (To save space, the diagram is not drawn to scale: each successive ring is supposed to be *vastly smaller* in relation to its including predecessor.)

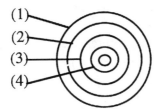

Now suppose that in actual fact the situation is as follows:

- Within circle (1) we have it that "Most A's are B's" because the larger part of this circle that lies outside (2) is heavily populated with A's that are B's.
- Within circle (2) we have it that "Most A's are not B's" because the larger part of the circle that lies outside (3) is heavily populated with A's that are not B's.
- Within circle (3) we have it that "Most A's are B's" because the larger part of this circle that lies outside (4) is heavily populated with A's that are B's.
- And so on in successive alternation.

Now suppose that we are informed (1) that we are dealing with an A which lies inside of circle (1). Then of course we would conclude that it is likely that this A is a B. But thereupon we are informed—additionally—that our A lies in circle (2). Then we will of course conclude, analogously, that it is not a B. But now suppose that we are informed additionally that our A lies in circle (3). Then, of course, the situation is restored to that of the outset and we will conclude that our A is likely to be a B. This sort of example suffices to demolish the idea that a conclusion based on fuller knowledge is thereby the more likely to be correct.

Throughout the realm of inductive or plausible reasoning, F & G can always point to a conclusion at odds with that indicated by F alone: the circumstance that fact F renders X highly probable is wholly compatible with the existence of another fact G of such a sort that F & G renders X highly improbable. And yet what G undermines here can always be restored by some yet further additional fact.

Precisely because additional knowledge always has the potential of constraining a change of mind—rather than merely providing additional substantiation for a fixed result—we have no assurance that further information produces "a closer approximation to the truth." Conclusions based on additional information may in some sense be comparatively "better" or "securer" but they need certainly not be "truer" or "more accurate." (There are no degrees here, true is true.)

5. Ignorance Can Have Its Compensations

One of the further ironies or our epistemic situation lies in the following consideration:

THESIS 6: *In many cases we may actually be better off by proceeding in ignorance—even in cognitive matters of belief formation.*

Consider the following situation:

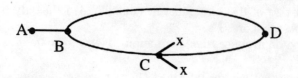

You need to go from A to D. And you know *nothing* about what will happen if you turn left at B. But suppose further that you know (quite correctly) that there actually is a possible way to get through to D if you turn right at B. But this is *all* that you know about this alternative—and, specifically, you have no information about the situation at C, where in fact two alternatives lead to disaster (x). In the circumstances you will (and should) conclude that you are more likely to succeed by turning right at B. The conclusion is sensible in the circumstances but quite incorrect. By opting for this alternative of a right turn at B you have a 2/3 probability of disaster and 1/3 probability of success. On the other hand, if you had lacked that item of knowledge regarding a right turn at B and had to proceed rationally in the absence of this datum—that is, by random selection—you would have had a 2/3 probability of success and a 1/3 probability of disaster. You are clearly better off—both epistemically and practically—lacking that (perfectly authentic) item of knowledge regarding the situation at B. For it actually reduces rather than enhances your chances of a correct resolution.

When we are seeking for the *true* answers to questions or for the *appropriate* resolution of choices the information or items of knowledge can, of course, prove to be *irrelevant*; so much is clear—and trivial. But what is equally clear and far less trivial is that—as we have seen—altogether true information can prove to be counterproductive and misleading. Additional information can serve to further skew an already biased picture. It can—all too easily—point perfectly sensible and rational people to the wrong conclusion even when proceeding by perfectly sensible and rational courses of inference. Accordingly, there are bound to be many sorts of situations in which people are better off without various items of knowledge—better off in ignorance, so to speak.

Given the way in which evidence works, and given that the evidence we have is our only cognitive accessory to reality, it can transpire that knowledge of truth can actually give us a very mistaken picture of reality. Truth is supposed to be "correspondence with reality" but the fact is that the truth can be misleading. This is brought out vividly in John Godfry Saxe's poem "The Blind Men and the Elephant" which tells the story of certain blind sages, those

> six men of Indostan,
> To learning much inclined,
> Who went to see the elephant,
> (Though all of them were blind).

One sage touched the elephant's "broad and sturdy side" and declared the beast to be "very like a wall." The second, who had felt its tusk, announced the elephant to resemble a spear. The third, who took the elephant's squirming trunk in his hands, compared it to a snake; while the fourth, who put his arm around the elephant's knee, was sure that the animal resembled a tree. A flapping ear convinced another that the elephant had the form of a fan; while the sixth blind man thought that is had the form of a rope, since he had taken hold of the tail.

> And so these men of Indostan,
> Disputed loud and long;
> Each in his own opinion
> Exceeding stiff and strong:
> Though each was partly in the right,
> And all were in the wrong.

None of those blind sages was altogether in error, it is just that the truth at their disposal was partial in a way that gave them a biased and misleading picture of reality. It is not that they did not know truth, but rather that an altogether plausible inference for the truth they knew propelled them into error.

And this sort of thing—bias—is a prospect whenever the information at our disposal is incomplete, which is to say virtually always. Conclusions based on incomplete information—and how often is it that our information is actually complete?—are always vulnerable, always in a condition where things can go wrong. And merely *increasing* information need not mend matters, seeing that "bigger" generally stops well short of "complete." In a world of almost inevitably incomplete information we always face the prospect that the further information we have managed to obtain simply leads us further down the primrose path towards an erroneous conclusion.

There is a natural tendency—among intellectuals in particular—to think of knowledge as invariably a good thing. Ironically, however, the awkward fact that additional knowledge can be counterproductive and misleading is something that one just cannot forget or ignore.[3]

6. The Cognitive Life Offers No Guarantees: It is a Matter of Calculated Risks

Our knowledge is always conditioned by ignorance: the questions we can answer are abutted by ones that we cannot. But often this just does not matter as much as one might think. Often—and indeed even generally—the sort of information we can get is good enough for the practical purposes that confront us. Were this not so we would not be here as thinkers who—thanks to evolution—are able to tell the tale.

In this imperfect world, we are not in general in a position to proceed in our operations from the absolute best as such, but only from the visible best that is at our disposal—"the best *available* (or *discernible*) reason." We have to content ourselves with doing "the *apparently* best thing"—the best that is determinable in the prevailing circumstances. But, the fact remains that what is rationally optimal need not be correct. Things all go wrong here. The problem about doing the rational thing—doing that which we sensibly suppose to be supported by the best reasons—is that we realize full well that our information, inevitably being incomplete, may well point us in the wrong direction. We can never secure advance assurance that what we don't know makes no difference. Facing this "predicament of reason" that reason itself may well guide us amiss the problem remains: Why should we act on the most promising visible alternative, when visibility is restricted to the limited horizons of our own potentially inadequate vantage-point?

The fact is that, like the drowning man, we clutch at the best available prospect. We recognize full well that even the most rationally laid scheme can misfire. Reality is not always and inevitably on the side of the strongest arguments. Reason affords no guarantee of success, but only the reassurance of having made the best rational bet—of having done as well as one could in the circumstances of the case. After all, this imperfect sublunary dispensation, probability is, as Bishop Butler said, "the guide of life." The rational person is, by definition, someone who uses intelligence to maximize the probability—that is, *the responsibly formed subjective probability*—that matters will eventuate favorably for the promotion of his real interests. It is exactly this that makes following the path of rationality the rational course. Rationality calls for adopting the overall best (visible) alternative—the best, that is, in practice, available to us in the circumstances.

Unfortunately, however, this is still not quite the end of it. For the problem remains: Exactly what are the probabilities with which we are operating? Of course, we *intend* them to be objective, real-world likelihoods; this is what we would ideally *like* to have. But, in fact, of course, they are no more than our considered *estimates* of such likelihoods as best we can shape them in the light of the available information. And this means that we are once again in the presence of rational resolutions effected on the basis of the *available* data. We are here confronted with an instant, local replay of the global problem that is being addressed. Striving to escape the predicament of reason, it mocks us by leaping ahead to bar our way. For we here confront once more the familiar and vexing issue of the actual optimality of apparent optima. And there is nothing we can do to escape this awkward circumstance—we simply have to take it in our stride.

The fact of the matter is that we cannot prove that rationality pays— that acting rationally in the particular case at hand will *actually* pay off—nor can we even claim with unalloyed assurance that it will *probably* do so (with real likelihood rather than subjective probability at issue). We can only say that, as best we can judge the matter, it represents the most promising course at our disposal. To reemphasize: We have no guarantees.

7. The Rationale of Rationality

So just where does this leave us? Actually it leaves us without any real choice—without any viable alternative. For there is nothing that we can reasonably do save to follow the guidance or reason.

But is this not to appoint reason as judge and jury in its own case? Yes—it actually is. But we would not—or *should* not!—want it any other way. For if we want any sort of guidance as to what to do, it is clearly rational guidance—guidance based on good reasons—that we do (and should) want.

Still, this is not quite the end of the matter. Of course, reason is self-recommending. The most rational course before us is to rely on reason. That goes without saying. But one further important thing can be said. For it is not just reason that speaks for reason, but experience as well. For experience teaches that in these cognitive matters reason is our best available guide. In the end we thus return full circle to the point offered in passing at the outset, that evolutionary considerations endorse our being reasonably confident that we live in a world where the guidance of reason serves us rational beings well. Of course in doing so we run the risk of error, but rational caution, being what it is, will do so on the whole in a way that keeps the odds on our side. After all, if rational comportment did not by and large pay off in terms of successful results then we would not be here as the (frequently) rational beings that we are. If rationality were not generally productive rather than counterproductive then the selective pressures of evolutionary survival would not have seen the emergence of rational creatures upon nature's stage.

Of course, one may somehow *prefer* not to be rational. With belief, I may prefer congeniality to truth. With action, I may prefer convenience to optimality. With value, I may prefer the pleasingly base to the more austere better. On all sides, I may willfully opt for "what I simply like," rather than for that which is normatively appropriate. But if I do this, I lose sight of the actual ends of the cognitive, practical, and evaluative enterprises, to the detriment of my *real* (as opposed to *apparent*) interests. It lies in the nature of things that reason is on the side of rationality. Admittedly, she offers us no guarantees. Yet, if we abandon reason there is nowhere better that we can (rationally) turn.[4] In the end, reason and pragmatism enter into a symbiotic cooperation.

And so, what makes the present discussion an exercise in contemplating *learned* ignorance is its recognition that, notwithstanding the very real advantages that it can bring, in the final analysis ignorance is not a good thing. The dictum that "Ignorance is bliss" does not get it right.[5]

Notes

1. Examples of this sort indicate why philosophers are unwilling to identify *knowledge* with *true belief*.
2. This circumstance did not elude Niels Bohr himself, the father of complementarity theory in physics:

   In later years Bohr emphasized the importance of complementarity for matters far removed from physics. There is a story that Bohr was once asked in German what is the quality that is complementary to truth (*Wahrheit*). After some thought he answered clarity (*Klarheit*). (Stephen Weinberg, *Dreams of a Final Theory* [New York: Pantheon Books, 1992], p. 74 footnote 10.)

3. The present deliberations have a deep kinship with the doctrines of Nicholas of Cusa. His classic *De docta ignorantia* pioneered the idea that knowledge can—and to some extent must—take root in ignorance. And his doctrine of "coincidence of opposites" also comes into the picture. However "coincidence" must here be understood not as total agreement (sameness) but in the sense of coming together, of being in contact or touch. It isn't the same thing to travel clockwise or counterclockwise in a circle, but eventually you'll reach the same point. Knowledge and ignorance are different things but in many cases one of them can be achieved through the mediation of its opposite.
4. This line of thought is developed from another point of departure in the author's *Rationality* (Oxford: Clarendon Press, 1988).
5. I am grateful to my colleague Richard Gale for constructive criticism.

7

Against Cognitive Relativism

1. What's Wrong with Relativism

Inquiry is an inevitably cooperative enterprise. We may stand on our own feet, but they never manage to find bedrock here, seeing that we always stand on the shoulders of others. Unfortunately, however, we live in an era of relativism. "To each his own" and "I did it my way" figure among the mottos of the day. In the prevailing circumstances, all too few of us manage to come to the realization that in cognitive matters this is a profoundly mistaken approach.

I think *X*, you think *Y*. I hold *A* to be correct, you opt for *B*. And this, as the cognitive relativist sees it, is simply the end of the matter. To refute such a position it must be shown that there is a sound basis for claiming that it is *not* the end of the matter. It has to be established that it is, or can be, the case that you should think as I do, and conversely, because certain beliefs represent the objectively right and appropriate thing to think.

It must be emphasized from the very outset that to ask for it to be shown that my view is the correct one is not to ask whether—and, if so, how—I can succeed in convincing you that my view is correct. It is not necessarily *you* that I need to convince here. Rather, it is the uninvolved, unprejudiced, reasonable bystander. It is in relation to such suitable third parties that the issue of cognitive appropriateness must be pursued. The real question is not what you or I *do* think but rather what, in the circumstances, anybody *ought* to think.

Ought you to think as I do? At this point we will have to take a

83

closer look at me. The pivotal question becomes one of how I proceed in matters of thinking. Clearly, if I am a frivolous, careless, sloppy thinker there is no reason why you should think as I do.

Now of course I can only manage to persuade those reasonable bystanders if I myself am reasonable about it. I cannot persuade them to go along with the idea of: "I think X, therefore you should think X as well" unless I can convince them to think it is reasonable for you to think X. And they will certainly not agree that others should think as I do if they do not accept that I am being reasonable about it.

I cannot, without further ado, plausibly take the line, "What I accept, everyone ought to accept." But, of course, I can, if I so choose, reverse matters here. That is, I can choose to heed the demands of objective reason by proceeding on the principle and policy of myself accepting just exactly that which anyone and everyone ought to accept in the circumstances. I can, in sum, be reasonable about this matter of acceptance.

What is now at issue is not the cognitive egomania of the idea "Everyone ought to think as I do" but the cognitive modesty of the idea "I ought to think as any reasonable person would in the circumstance." The line is not: "I think X and so you should do so too because you ought to be guided by me." Rather, it is: "I think X because it's the right think to do in the circumstances and *that's* the reason why you should think X too." It is precisely this policy that best accommodates the demands of impersonal reason. And of course if I proceed on this basis, then the approval of those who are—by hypothesis—*reasonable* bystanders is (ipso facto) assured.

The most promising prospect for refuting relativism accordingly lies in the recourse to reason. For rational acceptance carries with it an inherent claim to universality. The rational person accepts exactly what he is convinced that everyone *ought* to accept because accepting it is, in the circumstances, the rationally appropriate thing to do.

And so the idea "I think X, therefore you should think so too" is (or can be) sensible and acceptable—but only if I myself am rational by proceeding on the basis of seeking to accept only that which people-in-general ought to accept.

To be sure, when I think X and am appropriately convinced that you should think so too, I do not thereby revoke your right to think non-X. You are a free agent and are at liberty to do as you please. But this only means that I concede you the right to fall into error. And of course in granting you this right (in the sense of entitlement) I do not and need not think that it is right (in the sense of appropriate) that you should fall into error.

At this stage, an objector may well complain as follows: "You argumentation pivots on the principle 'if it is universally reasonable to think X then everyone should do so.' But you have given us no way of discerning or identifying that which it is reasonable to think. It is surely one thing to *claim* objective validity, and another actually to *achieve* it."

Here it must, of course, be acknowledged that we have no automatic process—no *mechanical algorithm*—for achieving cognitive adequacy. But the difficulty of attaining generality here does not mean that this desideratum is beyond our grasp in the various particular cases that confront us. It is certainly possible to produce examples of things every reasonable person could reasonably be expected to accept. Examples abound, witness Descartes' "I exist"; G. E. Moore's "This is a human hand"; Dr. Samuel Johnson's "This is a stone"; C. S. Peirce's "This stone will fall to the ground when I let go of it." Reasonable people are prepared to give credit to the "normal" sources of cognition. They can be expected to concede the ordinary presumptions· of truth, and we will certainly expect them to take the line "innocent until proven guilty" toward sources like the testimony of the senses and the reflections of commonsense thinking.

There are certainly no guarantees that matters will always turn out for the good—or, rather, for the true—when we do the reasonable thing in matters of belief. But experience indicates that we will then be right more often than not in doing so. And this is not only a matter of experience but of the inherent sense of things. For, after all, that right-indicative tendency is exactly the determinative function that makes for reasonableness in matters of belief.

2. What's Right with Objectivism

The preceding reflections provide a clear indication of what is wrong with relativism. For the relativist systematically takes the line that "There's no good reason to expect that you should think as I do." And this is just not sensible. For when my thinking proceeds as it ought—when it is grounded in what are standardly taken to be evidentially sound reasons—then this very fact constitutes a good reason why you

should think as I do. It is the factor of *objective cogency* that constitutes the crucial coordinating principle which links together the conclusions and acceptances of reasonable people.

But this line of thought still leaves some important open questions
on the agenda—in particular: What's right with objectivism? Why be
objective? To ask this is to ask for cogent reasons for cognitive objectivity. But of course there is no point in plunging into a discussion in
the setting of why-do-something questions if one is not going to cast
rationality to the winds here. So we have to construe "Why be objective?" as: Give me a good reason—an impersonally and objectively
good reason—for being objective. This circumstance alone suffices to
show that objectivity has to be respected even by those who are, for
reasons of their own, concerned to call it into question. It itself attests
the appropriateness of objectivity.

The next question is that of just what objectivity is all about. How
is one to understand what is involved here? To achieve a reasonable
approximation we shall suppose that, more or less by definition: To be
objective is to proceed as *any* reasonable person would do in the
circumstances at issue. But just how do reasonable persons comport
themselves? What does their reasonableness ask of them? The answer
here is that reasonable persons are optimizers—individuals who do the
best they can with the means available in the prevailing circumstances,
endeavoring to do that which is the best thing possible to do (in the
circumstances). And at this point, the answer to our initial question
lies before us clear and plain. For the very fact that something is the
best that can be done in this circumstance is ipso facto a good reason
for doing it—for anyone. And so the challenge "Why be objective?" is
resolved in a manifestly cogent way by the simple and straightforward
answer: Because it is the reasonable thing to do.

Rational belief, action, and evaluation are possibly only in situations where there are *cogent grounds* (and not just compelling personal motives) for what one does. And the cogency of grounds is a
matter of objective standards. The idea of rationality is in principle
inapplicable where one is at liberty to make up one's rules as one goes
along—effectively to have no predetermined rules at all. For a belief,
action, or evaluation to qualify as rational, the agent must (in theory at
least) be in a position to "give an account" of it on whose basis others
can see that "it is only right and proper" for him to resolve the issue in
that way.

Objectivity thus pivots on rationality. But the rationality at issue involves more than mere logical coherence. It is a matter of the intelligent pursuit of circumstantially appropriate objectives.[1] Accordingly its demands are few in type but elaborate in extent:

- aligning one's beliefs with the available evidence;
- maintaining consistency within one's beliefs;
- making reasonable efforts to ensure the adequacy of the available evidence to the problems at hand.

There is nothing idiosyncratic about such principles. What is evidence for one will have to count as evidence for another if *evidence* it indeed is. What is an authentically cogent inference with you is cogent inference with me. And so on.

The generality of access at issue with objectivity becomes crucial here. If something makes good rational sense, it must be possible in principle for anyone and everyone to see that this is so. This matter of good reasons is not something subjective or idiosyncratic; it is objective and lies in the public domain. There is no exclusively personalized rational cogency: what is cogent for me would be equally cogent for anyone in the circumstances. Robinson Crusoe may well proceed in a perfectly rational way in the context of his peculiar setting. But, he can only do so by doing what would make sense for others is similar circumstances. He must, in principle, be in a position to persuade others to adopt his course of action by an appeal to general principles to show them that his actions were appropriate in the circumstances. Rationality is thus inherently general and objective in its operations, endeavoring to deal with issues in an objective manner—in such a way that anyone can see the sense of it.

We thus have the core of the solution to our initial question of what is wrong with an objectivity dismissive relativism. The answer is that in cognitive matters relativism violates objectivity and objectivity violations are at odds with being reasonable.

Let us consider some of the ramifications of this position, and, in particular, the question of what it is that reasonableness and rationality demands.

3. Objectivity and the Circumstantial Universality of Reason

Consider the following contention: "There are no objective facts—or at least none that we can formulate by the use of language. For the man-made character of all our human contrivances means that everything that we can manage to produce is a cultural artifact within the course of human history in the setting of a particular place and time. And this is also emphatically the case with respect to our language and whatever we produce by its means, all of our statements, claims, and assertions included. How, then, can anything that people say possibly be wholly independent of all they—people that they are—think and believe? And even if some fact were to be something altogether objective and thought-independent, how can we ever get there from here?"

It is readily seen that what we have here is simply a mass of confusions. Thus take a shovel. It, too, is a cultural artifact made in the course of human history. But it can touch and move materials that are nowise man-made (earth and sand, say). Even so, statement are artifacts that can touch and handle facts that are nowise man-made (cats emplaced on mats, for example).

"No truths or purported truths are ever actually objective in the sense of being wholly independent of what people think or believe. Consider the (presumptive) fact that 'copper conducts electricity.' Clearly if people thought differently about the meaning of words—and specifically about the meaning of 'copper', say by letting it stand for what we call *wood*—then this would no longer be true."

This argument trades on a vitiating ambiguity. Two very different items are in play here, namely:

- copper-now = "copper" as now conceived
- copper-then = "copper" in its modified understanding

However true it might be to say that copper-then fails to conduct electricity, it would be patently false to say that copper-now fails to do so. Indeed the status of copper-now is entirely untouched by bringing copper-then upon the state of consideration. (It is, after all, the meaning of our present terminology as we actually have it and use it that is at issue in the communication we presently construe by its means.

"But if facts are something independent our human thoughts and beliefs—if they obtain irrespective of anything that we do in this mind-connected realm—then how can human thought and belief ever succeed in managing to consider, present, or convey them? How can thought come into (cognitive) contact with something entirely outside itself?"

To ask this is to be obtuse and foolishly closed-minded. It is like asking "Since numbers are nonphysical abstractions how can they ever be used to count sheep?" Numbers, by their very nature, are thought-accessible counting instruments that can be used throughout to enumerate collections of objects. Similarly statements are thought-accessible description instruments that can be used by thought to describe objective arguments in the world. That's simply how things work. If numbers couldn't be used to count real things they would not be what they are. And similarly if words, ideas, and concepts could not be used to characterize objectively real things, communication would be blocked at the starting gate.

"But surely when I say or think 'The cat is on the mat' I am managing to achieve no more than to avow 'I think/believe that the cat is on the mat.'" Wrong! These two remarks are very different. The one is something about the world (viz., that the cat is on the mat). The other is something about you and your thoughts (viz., that you think or believe that the cat is on the mat). And these are very different issues. And no sort of statement specifically about you and your beliefs can ever be equivalent with a claim regarding the you-independent arrangement of the world.

Objectivity is a matter of what one *ought* to think—that which is right and proper to think in the circumstances. And that little expression "in the circumstances" is critical to objectivity. For that which one ought to want *in the circumstances*—is exactly that which any sensible person should—and as *sensible* person would—think if they were "in one's shoes," that is, if the circumstances were the same. Of course, different people are differently situated and this is something that rationality requires us to take into account. It is only the deeply underlying "fundamental principles" that are uniform. In this sense, reason plays no favorites, for while people's circumstances differ—vastly and endlessly—nevertheless that which is reasonable for X in his (X's) circumstances is ipso facto also reasonable for anyone who is (or would be) situated in the *relevantly* identical circumstances.

To be sure, it must be granted to relativists that, as William James insisted, "There is no point of view absolutely public and universal."[2]

The "God's eye view" on things is unavailable—at any rate to us. Whatever we can judge we must judge from the vantage point of a position in space, time, and cultural context. But, of course, it is not the absoluteness of an unrealizable point of view from nowhere or from everywhere-at-once or from God's vantage point that is at issue with objectivity. Objectivity is a matter of how we *should* proceed— and how otherwise reasonable people *would* proceed if they were in our shoes in the relevant regards. It is a matter of doing not what is impossible but what is appropriate.

Reason is (circumstantially) universal, and it is objectivity's coordination with rationality that links it to universality. That which (as best one can tell) is the sensible thing for us to do in the circumstances is thereby the reasonable thing for *anybody*—any rational individual—to do *in those circumstances*. The objectivity at issue accordingly comes down to rationality. If it is reasonable for you to *A* in circumstance *X*, then it is so for anybody else—and conversely. Reason is agent-indifferent.

The principles operative in the rational economy of things are all objective and universal—though of course their application will bear differently on differently situated individuals. What it was rational for Galen to believe—given the cognitive "state of the art" of his day regarding medical matters—is in general no longer rational for us to believe today. Obviously, what it is rational for someone to do or to think *hinges on the particular details of how this individual is circumstanced*—and the prevailing circumstances of course differ from person to person and group to group. To be objective in one's proceedings is to do what any sensible person would do in one's place and we don't all stand on the same spot. The resolution of an issue is objective if it is arrived at without the introduction of any resources (be they substantive or methodological) that would not be deemed as acceptable *in the circumstances* by any rational and reasonable individual. Accordingly, the rulings of rationality are universal, alright, but conditionally universal, indeed subject to a person-relativity geared to the prevailing conditions. This sort of contextualism does not engender corrosive do as you please "relativism," but represents a deep central fact about our procedural situation. To reemphasize: rationality is universal alright, but it is *circumstantially* universal.

To be sure, we cannot shed our individuality like a snake its skin. Be it in cognitive, practical, or evaluative matters, rationality has two distinguishable but inseparable aspects, the one personal, private, and particular, the other impersonal, public, and universal. The private (particularized) aspect turns on what is advisable *for the agent*, duly considering his own personal situation in point of his circumstances— his opportunities, capabilities, talents, objective, aspirations, values, needs, and wants. (Note that we here construe "circumstances" very broadly, including not only the outer and situational, but also the inner conditions that relate to a person's physical and psychological make-up.) The universalized aspect of rationality turns on its being advisable by person-indifferent and objectively cogent standards for *anyone in those circumstances* to do the "rationally appropriate" things at issue. The standards of rational cogency are general in the sense that what is rational for one person is also rational for others—but here we have to add: for those others who are *in his shoes*. Both aspects, the situational and the universal, are inseparable facets of rationality as we standardly conceive it.

But what about this "in my place" business? What can they bring along in getting there! What those others can bring along and what of mine are they allowed to displace? Clearly what they are bringing along is their rationality, and reasonableness, their common sense and good judgment. But my circumstances and conditions, my commitments and interests are things they have to leave in place. Clearly they are not to substitute their predilections and preferences, their values and affinities for mine, their beliefs and desires for mine. *Everything* must remain as was except for those characteristics that go against the dictates of reason: phobias, groundless anxieties, delusions, senseless antipathies, and irrationalities of all sorts. These must be erased, so to speak—and left blank. In making that suppositional transfer, one has to factor out all those psychic aberrations that stand in the way of a person's being sensible or reasonable.

The circumstances of human life are such that, like it or not, we need knowledge to guide our actions and to satisfy our curiosity. Without knowledge-productive inquiry we cannot resolve the cognitive and practical problems that confront a rational creature in making its way in this world. But in matters of knowledge production life is too short for us to proceed on our own. We simply cannot start at square one and do everything needful by ourselves. We must—and do—proceed in the setting of a larger community that extends across the reaches of time (via its cultural traditions) and space (via its social organization).

This requires communication, coordination, collaboration. And so even as the pursuit of objectivity is aided by an agent's recourse to the resources of the environing community, so conversely, is objectivity an indispensably useful instrumentality for the creation and maintenance of intercommunicative community. For there can be no community where people do not understand one another, and it is the fact that I endeavor to proceed as any rational person would in my place that renders my proceedings efficiently intelligible to others. The commonality of rational procedure provides the crucial coordination mechanism that renders people understandable to one another. It is, accordingly, a key instrumentality that positions each of us to benefit by a mutually advantageous commerce that is indispensable for the cooperation and collaboration without which our cognitive enterprise—and other social enterprises in general—would be infeasible.

4. Objectivity and the Complexity of the First Person Plural

Proceeding with a view to objectivity in its impersonal mode is thus generally in our best interests. But is it not just advantageous but somehow obligatory? Objectivity's bonding to rationality shows that this is indeed the case. For insofar as we reason-capable agents have an obligation to exercise this capacity—as we indeed do—we are involved in a venture that carries the obligation to objectivity in its wake.[3] Let us see how this is so.

The subjectivity/objectivity contrast turns on the distinction between what is *accepted by me* as things stand—and quite possibly by me alone—over against that which is *acceptable for us* in general in suitably similar conditions. And this issue of a range of cogency pivots on the I/we contrast. The crucial contrast is that between what simply holds for oneself versus what is to be seen as holding for all of us. Objectivity is coordinate with generality: what is objectively so holds independently of the vagaries, contingencies, and idiosyncrasies of particular individuals.

Consider, in particular, the objectivity of claims and contentions. An objective truth does not hold *of* everyone; it holds *for* everyone. "Bald men have little or no hair" wears on its very sleeve the fact that it holds only *of* some—viz. of bald men. But it holds *for* everyone, is just as true for you as for me. The questions "who realizes it?" or "who has reason to believe it" certainly arise—and may well be answered by saying that only some people do so and many others don't. But the question "Whom is it true for?" simply does not arise in that form. If that contention is true at all, it is true for everyone. Truths do not need to be *thematically* universal and they do not need to be *evidentially* universal; but they do need to be universal in point of *validity*. And this precisely is the basis of their objectivity. As truths they will necessarily have that for-everyone aspect.

Objectivity keeps us on the straight and narrow path of commitments that are binding on all rational beings alike. But cultivating objectivity is certainly no exercise in power-projection. It is not a matter of trying to speak for others, preempting their judgment by a high-handedness that constrains them into alignment with oneself. Quite to the contrary, it works exactly the other way around. The proper pursuit of cognitive objectivity calls for trying to put one's own judgment into alignment with what—as best one can determine it—the judgment of those others ought to be. It is not a matter of coordination by an imposition upon others but the very reverse, one of a coordination by self-subordinated submission to the modus operandi of the group upon granting it the benefit of the doubt in point of rationality. Such conformity is a requisite for objectivity but the matter of how it comes about is pivotal. It is—and must be—a matter of my conforming to them (the generality of sensible people) as opposed to any megalomaniacal insistence that they conform to me. Objectivity is a policy not of the dictatorial but of the cognitively gregarious who seek to be in cognitive harmony with the rest—at least insofar as they subscribe to the standards of rationality.

The impetus to rationality accordingly has important and immediate implications for our concern with objectivity. For rationality carries objectivity in its wake: the universality and impersonality of reason validates the pursuit of objectivity in direct consequence. Objectivity's insistence on resolutions that are sensible and reasonable—that prevent the course of reason from being deflected by wish and willfulness, biases and idiosyncrasies—automatically foster and implement a commitment to the primacy of reason.

To proceed objectively is, in sum, to render oneself perspicuous to others by doing what any reasonable and normally constituted person would do in one's place, thereby rendering one's proceedings intelligible to anyone. When the members of a group are objective, they secure great advantages thereby: they lay the groundwork for community by paving the way for mutual understanding, communication, collaboration. And in cognitive matters they also sideline sources of error. For the essence of objectivity lies in its factoring out of those of one's idiosyncratic predilections and prejudices that would stand in the way of other intelligent people's reaching the same result. Objectivity follows in rationality's wake because of its effectiveness as a means to averting both isolation and error.

5. Other Cultures

But can objectivity manage to achieve a universalized impersonality? Can we expect other cultures to conform to our standards? Do not those other cultures have their own way of doing things—and thus also their own rationality?

Anthropologists, and even, alas, philosophers, often say things like "The Wazonga tribe has a concept of rationality different from ours, seeing that they deem it rationally appropriate (or even mandatory) to attribute human illness to the intervention of the rock-spirits."[4] But there are big problems here; this way of talking betokens lamentably loose thinking. For, compare:

(1)   The Wazonga habitually (customarily) attribute...
(2)   The Wazonga think it acceptable (or perhaps even necessary) to attribute...
(3)   The Wazonga think it rationally mandatory to attribute...

Now, however true and incontestable the first two contentions may be, the third is untenable. For compare (3) with

(4)   The Wazonga think is *mathematically* true that dogs have tails.

No matter how firmly convinced the Wazonga may be that dogs have tails, thesis (4), taken as a whole, remains a thesis *of ours*, and *not* of theirs! Accordingly, it is in deep difficulty unless the (highly implausible) condition is realized that the Wazonga have an essentially correct conception of what is, and, moreover, are convinced that the claim that dogs have tails belongs among the appropriate contentions of this particular realm. Analogously, one cannot appropriately maintain (3) unless one is prepared to claim both that the Wazonga have an essentially correct conception of what rationality is (correct, that is, by our lights), and furthermore that they are convinced that the practice in question is acceptable within the framework of this rationality project. And this concatenation is highly implausible in the circumstances.

The fact is that different cultures do indeed implement a rational principle like "Be in a position to substantiate your claims" very differently. (For one thing, there are different standards as to what constitutes proper "substantiation".) But, they cannot simply abandon such a characterizing principle of rationality. For if they were to convert to "It's all right to maintain anything that suits your fancy" they would not have a *different* mode of cognitive rationality but rather, in this respect at any rate, are simply *deficient* in cognitive rationality.

The anthropological route to a relativism of rationality, is, to say the least, highly problematic. There is no difficulty whatever about the idea of different belief systems, but the idea of different *rationalities* faces insuperable difficulties. The case is much like that of saying that the tribe whose counting practices are based on the sequence: "one, two, many" has a different arithmetic from ourselves. To do anything like justice to the facts one would have to say that they do not have *arithmetic* at all—but just a peculiar and very rudimentary way of counting. And similarly with the Wazonga. On the given evidence, they do not have a *different* concept of rationality, but rather, their culture has not developed to the point where they have any *conception* of rationality whatsoever. Rationality is, after all, a definite sort of enterprise with a characteristic goal structure of its own—the pursuit of appropriate ends by appropriate means. Its defining principles make for an inevitable uniformity.

To be sure, the question "What is the rational thing to believe or to do?" must receive the indecisive answer: "That depends." It depends on context and situation—on conditions and circumstances. At the level of the question "What is rational; what is it that should be believed or done?" a many-sided and pluralistic response is called for. The way in which people proceed to give a rational justification of something—be it a belief, action, or evaluation—is unquestionably variable and culture relative. We mortal men cannot speak with the tongues of angels. The means by which we pursue our ends in the setting of any major project—be it rationality, morality, communication, or nourishment—are "culture dependent" and "context variable." But the fact remains that certain crucial uniformities are inherent in the very nature of the projects in which we are engaged. With rationality as with swimming, different cultures and different people may go at it differently but the object of the enterprise is uniformly the same, fixed by the definitive conception of what is at issue.

6. Abandoning Objectivity is Pragmatically Self-Defeating

"I believe (accept, am convinced) that p" simply does not convey the same information as p. And neither does "Everybody is convinced and accepting of p." Language, as we use it, is simply at odds with relativistic subjectivism. In making a statement we implicitly assert that it is a matter of objective fact.

Sometimes we are told: "People never really know anything really and objectively: there is only what people think they know." But this contention is deeply problematic. Asserting "There are no objective facts" is self-contradictory. Whoever makes (asserts) this statement is presumably stating a matter of objective fact: they are not saying that they merely think it to be so.

What is at issue in an overt denial of facts is not a logical inconsistency but a practical inconsistency. For now the practice in which you are engaging becomes infeasible through the very nature of the way in which you are engaging in it. That is, you are engaging in a process of communication but doing it with a machine that produces a monkey wrench which it inserts into its own works.

Thoroughly practical (functional/operations) reasons thus speak on behalf of endorsing the conception of objective truth. Specifically we require it:

1. As a presupposition to make communication possible by way of agreement and disagreement. To principle a commonality of focus.
2. As a contrast conception that enables us to acknowledge our own potential fallibility.
3. As a regulative ideal whose pursuit stops us from resting content with too little.
4. As an entryway into a communicative community in which we acknowledge that our own views are nowise decisive.

The commitment to objectivity thus affords us an effective practical instrumentality that facilitates communication and cognitive collaboration. It is certainly not something that we have to endorse only "on faith." Practical experience amply endows it with a track record of utility that constitutes a retrospective justification of a commitment to objectivity. Its substantiation lies largely in the fact that we simply could not get on without it.

7. The Charge of Circularity

There is, of course, bound to be a skeptic who comes along to press the following objection: "Your proposed universalistic legitimation of objectivity pivots on the appropriateness of rationality. But your legitimation of reason conforms to the pattern: 'You should be rational just because that is the rational thing to do!' And this is clearly circular." It might seem questionable to establish the jurisdiction of reason by appeal to the judgment of reason itself. But, in act, of course, this circularity is not really vicious at all. Vicious circularity stultifies by "begging the question"; virtuous circularity merely coordinates related elements in their mutual interlinkage. The former presupposes what is to be proved, the latter simply shows how things are connected in a well-coordinated and mutually supportive interrelationship. The self-reliance of rationality merely exemplifies this latter circumstance of an inherent co-ordination among its universe components. It is not a matter of sequential validation but rather of a legitimation process that is coordinative and coherentistic.

Admittedly, the reasoning at issue has an *appearance* or vitiating circularity because the force of the argument itself rests on an appeal to rationality: "If you are going to be rational in your beliefs, then you must also act rationally, because it is rational to believe that rational action is optimal in point of goal attainment." But this sort of question begging is simply *unavoidable* in the circumstances. It is exactly what we want and need. Where else should we look for a *rational* validation of rationality but to reason itself? The only reasons for being rational that it makes sense to ask for are *rational* reasons. In this epistemic dispensation, we have no way of getting at the facts directly, without the epistemic detour of securing grounds and reasons for them. And it is, or course, rationally cogent grounds and reason that we want and need. The overall justification of rationality *must* be reflexive and self-referential. To provide a rationale of rationality is to show that rationality stands in appropriate alignment with the principles of rationality. From the angle of justification, rationality is a cyclic process that closes in on itself, not a linear process that ultimately rests on something outside itself.

There is, accordingly, no ground for any rational discontent, no room for any dissatisfaction or complaint regarding such a supposedly objectionable "circular" justification of rationality. We would not (should not) want it otherwise. If we bother to want an answer to the question 'Why be rational' at all, it is clearly a *rational* answer that we require. The only sort of justification of anything—rationality included—that is worth having at all is a rational one. That presupposition of rationality is not vitiating, not viciously circular, but essential—an unavoidable consequence of the self-sufficiency of cognitive reason. There is simply no satisfactory alternative to using reason in its own defense. Already embarked on the sea of rationality, we want such assurance as can not be made available that we have done the right thing. And such reassurance can indeed be given—exactly along the lines just indicated. Given the very nature of the justificatory enterprise at issue, one simply cannot avoid letting rationality sit in judgment on itself. (What is being asked for, after all, is a rational argument for rational action, a basis for rational conviction, and not persuasion by something probatively irrelevant like threats of force majeure.) One would expect, nay *demand*, that rationality be self-substantiating in this way—that it *must* emerge as the best policy on its own telling.

From the justifactory point of view, rationality is and must be autonomous. It can be subject to no external authority. Rationality in general is a matter of systematization, and the justification of rationality is, correspondingly, a matter of systemic self-sufficiency. Rather than indicating the defect of vicious circularity, the self-referential character of a justification of rationality is a precondition of its adequacy! It is *only* a rational legitimation of rationality that we would want; any other sort would avail us nothing. And if such a rational validation were not forthcoming this would indicate a grave defect.

To be sure, some theorists would see rationality as heteronomous—as subject to some external sort of authority such as "feeling" or "the will." Thus, one contemporary philosopher offers the idea that

[U]nderlying each…judgment there is a choice that the agent has made—a type of choice in which the individual is at the most fundamental level unconstrained by good reasons, precisely because his or her choice expresses a decision as to what is to count as a good reason for him or her.[5]

Such a view sees rational justification as linear and regressive—and thus as ultimately having to rest on an unrationalized rock-bottom that itself lies quite outside the domain of reason as a matter of ultimately unreasoned selection. But any such view is profoundly mistaken. For rational validation need *not* be linear and regressive; it can—quite appropriately—be rather cyclical and systemically self-contained. We need not—must not—subscribe to the Rock-Bottom Fallacy. There is no way of grounding good reasons in arbitrary or otherwise unrationalizable decisions. ("Deciding as to what is to count as a good reason" forsooth! Not even God is in a position to do that!)[6]. It makes no sense to ask "who gets to decide what it is rational for an agent to do?" In these factual matters there simply is no one who "gets to decide"—any more than someone "gets to decide" that 2 + 2 yields 4 or sunlight is brighter than moonlight. No one *decides* what sorts of things are to count as good reasons. This is something we cannot make up but only discover or learn. And in general, we only learn in the school of bitter experience what qualifies as such.

A desperate objection yet remains: "So rationality speaks on its own behalf. Well and good. But why should I care for rationality? Why should I set myself to do the intelligent and appropriate thing?"

At this point there is little more to be said. The preceding considerations already do the job insofar as it is doable. For if I want a reason at all, then I must—if I am being reasonable about it—want a *rational* reason. If I care about reasons at all, I am already within the project of rationality. But once I am *within* the project, there is nothing *further* external to reason that can *or need* be said to validate it. At *that* stage rationality is already at hand to provide its own support—it wears its justification on its sleeve. (The project of trying to reason with someone who stands *outside* the range of rationality to convince them to come into its fold is clearly an exercise in pointlessness and futility.)

A pervasive irrationalism is astir in the world that rejects the quest for rationally validated reasons and advocates a free-wheeling "anything goes"—even in the cognitive sphere of empirical inquiry.[7] But, of course, any sensible person who is not already committed to such a position would want to know if there is any good reason for taking it. And then we are at once back in the sphere of rationality and good reasons.

One may of course quite appropriately ask questions like: "Why should I cultivate the truth; why should I cultivate my best (or true) interests?" But in the very act of posing such questions I am asking for reasons—that is, I am evincing my commitment to the project of rationality. Caring for the truth and for one's best interests are simply part and parcel of this commitment. And if I do not care for these things, then there is really no point in raising these questions. Here we confront a lost cause. For if I take this line then I have *already* taken my place outside the precincts of rationality, beyond the reach of reason. And then, of course, there is no reason why any sensible person would want to follow me there.

And so it is, in the end, the fact that objectivity rides on the back of reason itself that provides it with a safe and secure transit to the domain of what is rationally justified.[8]

Notes

1. For an elaborate development of this position see the author's *Rationality: A Philosophical Inquiry into the Nature and the Rationale of Reason* (Oxford: Clarendon Press, 1988).
2. William James, *Talks to Teachers on Psychology* (New York: Henry Holt, 1899), p. 4.
3. On our duty towards the cultivation of rationality see also pp. 204–9 of the author's *Rationality*.
4. On "alternative standards of rationality" see Peter Winch, "Understanding a Primitive Society," *American Philosophical Quarterly*, 1 (1964), 307–24.
5. Alasdair MacIntyre, in MacIntyre and Stanley Haverwas (eds.), *Revisions* (Notre Dame: University of Notre Dame Press, 1983), p. 9.
6. On this point, see G. W. Leibniz's correspondence with Antoine Arnauld regarding the *Discourse on Metaphysics*.
7. See e. g., Paul K. Feyerabend, *Against Method* (New York: New Left Books, 1975).
8. This chapter is an expanded version of a keynote address delivered at the annual meeting of the West Virginia Philosophical Society in Charleston, West Virginia in October of 1997. Some relavant issues were also treated in the author's *Objectivity* (Notre Dame: University of Notre Dame Press, 1997).

8

Conclusion

The key overall lesson of these deliberations is that inquiry is a dynamical and ultimately incompletable process so that the agenda of questions and the inventory of our answers to them are not something stable but rather manifest an ever-continuing flux. The project of resolving our questions, in science as elsewhere, is developmental and open-ended as new issues arise and old ones drop from sight. Experience teaches that natural science is by its very nature self-destabilizing and for this very reason cannot be cognitively tethered, limited, completed—or indeed predicted.

In exploring this terrain, the theses of the book are woven together in a way which makes for a coherent overall story that runs essentially as follows: Knowledge is not the only key theme of epistemology because in the realm of cognition questions are every bit as important as answers (chapter 1). Questions have a rational dynamic of their own that cannot be grasped if we look simply to their product—the inherently imperfectable knowledge that issues from our efforts to resolve them (chapters 2–3). Inquiry is a dynamical process and the phenomenon of question exfoliation is one of its crucial features (chapter 4). While we cannot define scientific progress by purely theoretical means, strictly cognitive, problem-solving terms, we can indeed characterize it in *practical* terms of technological capacity. In this (technological) manner science indeed can and does progress; it can always do more and do better, and that its practical capacity is indeed cumulative. However, it makes no sense to think of its doing *everything*. In this realm completion and perfection are just not in the cards (chapter

5). Nevertheless, the very fact that we are here, have evolved in the world as an information-guided creature shows that the sort of knowledge we can get—however imperfect—is good enough for our practical purposes (chapter 6). All the same, the cognitive project as we do—and should—pursue it commits us to the quest for the objective truth. However difficult the path of objectivity may be, its abandonment would exact an unacceptable price from us (chapter 7).

In detailing this account of rational inquiry, the book has highlighted a substantial series of fundamental principles of question epistemology:

- *Question-answer coordination* (chapter 2): Questions and answers stand coordinate with one another.
- *Potential question dissolution* (chapter 3): Scientific questions are frequently impermanent.
- *State-of-the-art stages* (chapter 4): A state of science can be identified uniquely either via its question agenda or via its manifold of answers.
- *Kant's principle of question exfoliation* (chapter 4): Rational inquiry is self-perpetuating: "Every state of knowledge raises new questions which it itself is not, as yet, able to answer."
- *Progress as growth of practical capacity* (chapter 5): Various suggestions have been made on how to understand scientific progress in terms of question-answer relationships. Progress, it has been said, consists in answering more questions, or posing more questions, or in increasing the proportion of answered (or perhaps of unanswered) questions, or the like. No such thing can be substantiated. Scientific progress is not something that can be discerned by purely theoretical reflections regarding questions and answers. It is a matter of technological enhancement: Every new and improved state of science possibilizes certain practical accomplishments that were impracticable heretofore.
- *The veniality of ignorance* (chapter 6): The inability to answer all of our questions is an inevitable reality of the human condition. However, evolutionary considerations afford us good reason to think that we live in a user-friendly world where we do not need to be right about things for our opinion-guided action to be successful.
- *The quest for truth* (chapter 7): Nevertheless we have every reason to pursue the cognitive project energetically with an assured confidence that the game is worth the candle.

What lessons do such abstract considerations of general principle have for the working scientist? Only a few—and these of a general import. They run as follows: Realize that a state of science is always and inevitably the artifact of an era. Recognize that even at best "thou art but mortal" and natural science of your time always involves an element of fallibility—it is capable of being refined, extended, improved, and in various respects, superseded. But bear in mind that it is exactly because no one can impose on you the burden of definitive finality that you are free to take calculated risks and to venture into the realm of reasonable conjectures.

No doubt these injunctions represent common-sense fundamentals that the working scientist generally divines by instinct. Yet only good can come of having them confirmed and substantiated through an explicit reflection on basic principles. It is, after all, through considered reflection on the theoretical ramifications and limitations of inquiry dynamics that we can best form a sensible view of the cognitive enterprise. For in its absence we are open to unrealistic expectations that can lead to nothing but disillusion and unjustified discouragement.

Summary of Notation and Symbols

The symbolic machinery employed in the discussion (over and above the usual notation of symbolic logic) is as follows:

- *Questions*: Q, Q', etc.

- *Problems*: P, P', etc.

- *Answers/solutions/statements*: $p, q, r,\ldots$

- *Bodies of knowledge*: $K, K_1, K_2\ldots$

- *Times*: $t, t', t'',\ldots$, also n for *now*

- *States of science*: $S, S',\ldots, S_t$ (= the state of science at time t)

- *Possible answers*
  $\alpha(Q) =_{df}$ the set of possible explicit answers to $Q = \{p: p$ affords a possible answer to $Q\}$

- *Presuppositions*
  $Q \ni p =_{df} (\forall q)[q \in \alpha(Q) \to (q \to p)]$

- *Proper questions*
  $prop(Q) =_{df} (\forall p)[(Q \ni p) \to p]$

- *Permanent questions*
  $perm(Q) =_{df} (\exists t)(\forall t' > t)(Q \in K_t)$

- *Propositional answers*
  $p@Q =_{df} p \& p \in \alpha(Q)$

- *Body-of-knowledge answerability*
  $K @ Q =_{df} (\exists p)(p \ni K \,\&\, p @ Q)$

- *Question sets*
  $Q(K) =_{df} \{Q : (\forall p)[(Q \ni p) \supset (p \in K)]\}$

- *Answer sets* $Q^*(K) =_{df} \{Q : Q \in Q(K) \,\&\, K @ Q\}$

- *Explanatory answers*
  $p \, \Sigma \, q =_{df} p$ is a fact that plays a primary, predominating role in the correct answer to an explanatory question of the form: "Why is q the case?"

Name Index